Brief Motivational Interviewing for Busy Clinicians

The 10-Minute OARS Framework for Primary Care, Health Coaching, and Behavior Change Conversations

Andrew Arthur Peanut

A structured, evidence-based clinical guide with fourteen chapters, twenty practice scenarios, nine pre-built scripts, reproducible pocket tools, and a complete OARS toolkit for time-constrained encounters.

First Edition

ISBN: 978-1-7645936-5-6

Table of Contents

Preface

Every clinician has had the same conversation a hundred times. The lab results are on the screen. The patient is in the chair. The numbers say something needs to change. And so the clinician explains, advises, recommends, warns, encourages, and ultimately watches the patient nod politely and leave the office to do exactly what they were doing before.

That conversation has a name in the motivational interviewing literature. It is called the righting reflex: the instinct to fix what appears broken by telling the person what to do. It is well-intentioned. It is clinically logical. And it fails, consistently, across virtually every health behavior and every patient population studied. Decades of research have confirmed what most clinicians already sense in their gut: information alone does not produce behavior change. If it did, no physician would smoke, no nurse would skip breakfast, and no health coach would be sedentary. Human motivation is not a knowledge problem. It is a conversation problem.

Motivational interviewing, developed by William R. Miller and Stephen Rollnick beginning in 1983, was designed to solve that conversation problem. It replaces the clinician-as-expert model with a collaborative model in which the patient's own values, goals, and language become the engine of change. The evidence base is substantial. Meta-analyses spanning thousands of studies demonstrate that MI produces small to moderate but reliable improvements across smoking cessation, medication adherence, physical activity, alcohol reduction, chronic disease self-management, and a broad range of other health behaviors. These effects are present even in brief interventions of one to three sessions, many lasting fifteen minutes or less.

The challenge has never been the evidence. The challenge has been the implementation. MI was developed and taught in the context of extended therapeutic sessions. The foundational texts, brilliant as they are, run to four hundred pages. The training workshops span multiple days. And the average primary care visit lasts fifteen to twenty minutes, with the behavior-change portion compressed into a fraction of that time. The result is a paradox: the clinicians who most need MI, those working in high-volume, time-constrained settings where behavior-change conversations happen dozens of times per day, are the least likely to have the time to learn it.

This book was written to close that gap. It compresses the core principles, skills, and strategies of motivational interviewing into a structured, clock-based template that fits inside a ten-minute encounter. The template is not a script. It is a scaffold: flexible enough to adapt to any patient and any setting, but structured enough to ensure that every minute counts. Four phases, OPEN, FOCUS, EVOKE, PLAN, map directly onto MI's four processes and provide clear guidance on what to do, what to say, and when to transition.

The first half of the book teaches the foundations: MI's spirit, the OARS communication skills, change talk and sustain talk recognition, and the evidence supporting brief MI. The second half applies the template across primary care, health coaching, dental, pharmacy, emergency medicine, pediatrics, and integrated behavioral health. The final chapters address skill development, team implementation, and long-term practice sustainability. The appendices provide every reproducible tool a clinician needs: a one-page consult sheet, pocket reference cards, twenty scored clinical practice scenarios, pre-built scripts for nine common topics, a self-assessment scorecard, and a complete glossary.

The premise is simple. Meaningful, evidence-based conversations about behavior change do not require an hour. They require a framework, a set of skills, and the discipline to use them consistently. The ten-minute conversation will not transform every patient encounter. But practiced daily, across weeks and months and years, it will change the nature of clinical relationships. And those relationships are where the real work of health improvement begins.

How to Use This Book

You are holding a book designed for people who do not have time to read books.

That sounds like a contradiction, and in most cases it would be. But this book was built with a specific promise in mind: everything you need to conduct a meaningful, motivational conversation in ten minutes or less is contained within these pages, organized so you can find it fast, use it today, and come back to it again and again without rereading a single chapter.

Here is the structure. The book is divided into two halves and a set of appendices.

The first half, Parts One and Two, teaches you what you need to know. Part One covers the foundations of motivational interviewing: what it is, where it came from, how its core skills work, and why it is effective even in brief encounters. Part Two introduces the 10-Minute MI Template, walks you through each phase of the framework, and prepares you for the real-world complications that will inevitably arise. If you read these seven chapters once, carefully, you will have the conceptual foundation to practice brief MI with confidence.

The second half, Parts Three and Four, shows you how to apply the framework in specific settings and how to build lasting skill. Part Three covers primary care, diet and exercise, health coaching, and a range of additional clinical environments from emergency departments to dental offices. Part Four addresses self-directed skill building, team implementation, and long-term practice maintenance. These chapters are designed for selective reading. Go to the chapter that matches your setting or your current challenge.

The appendices are your everyday toolkit. Appendix A contains the One-Page Consult Sheet, which is the single most important page in this book. It distills the entire 10-minute template onto one reproducible sheet that you can laminate, tape to your computer monitor, or slip into your coat pocket. Appendix B provides the OARS Quick-Reference Card. Appendix C offers a Change Talk recognition guide. Appendix D contains twenty clinical scenarios for practice. The remaining appendices include self-assessment tools, pre-built scripts for common topics, and a glossary. These tools are designed to be photocopied, printed, and used in your daily clinical workflow.

Every chapter follows the same internal pattern. Each one opens with a brief clinical scenario, a short vignette drawn from the kind of encounter you might face on any given Tuesday afternoon. The scenario is not there for decoration. It is there to anchor every concept that follows in something concrete and recognizable. Each chapter closes with a Pocket Summary, a condensed, one-page version of the chapter's most essential content. The pocket summaries are formatted for quick reference. Think of them as the notes you would write in the margin if you were studying for an exam, except they are already written for you.

The design philosophy of this book can be summarized in four words: read once, reference forever. You do not need to reread Chapter 3 every time you want to remember how reflective listening works. You read it once, absorb the ideas, and then use the OARS Cheat Sheet in Appendix B whenever you need a refresher. You do not need to reread Chapter 5 before every patient encounter. You read it once, internalize the template, and then glance at the One-Page Consult Sheet whenever you need to recalibrate.

A note on what this book is not. It is not a replacement for Miller and Rollnick's foundational text, Motivational Interviewing: Helping People Change and Grow. That book is the field's definitive resource, and if you are serious about deepening your MI practice, you should read it. What this book offers instead is a bridge. It connects the evidence base and the principles of MI to the operational realities of modern clinical work, where visits are short, patients are complex, and the temptation to simply give advice is constant. If Miller and Rollnick wrote the theory, this book writes the playbook.

One final note. You will notice that this book consistently uses the word "patient" in clinical examples and "client" in coaching examples. Both terms refer to the person sitting across from you. Use whichever word fits your practice. The skills are the same.

Welcome to the ten-minute conversation that can change everything.

PART ONE: FOUNDATIONS (WHY BRIEF MI WORKS)

Chapter 1.0: The Ten-Minute Problem

Dr. Amara Hassan glanced at the schedule on her screen and felt the familiar tightening in her chest. Fourteen patients before lunch. Mr. Delgado, her next appointment, was a 58-year-old man with type 2 diabetes, elevated blood pressure, and a hemoglobin A1C that had been climbing steadily for two years. His last three visits had followed the same pattern: she reviewed his labs, explained why his numbers were concerning, recommended dietary changes and more consistent medication use, and watched him nod politely before leaving with no discernible change in behavior. The entire behavior-change portion of their visit typically lasted about three minutes. She knew it was not enough. She also knew she did not have more to give.

Dr. Hassan's experience is not unusual. It is, in fact, the norm. Across primary care, urgent care, dental practices, pharmacy counters, and telehealth platforms, clinicians face the same structural problem: the conversations that matter most for long-term health outcomes are squeezed into the smallest available windows of time. The question that drives this book is deceptively simple. Is it possible to have a meaningful, evidence-based conversation about behavior change in ten minutes or less? The answer, supported by three decades of research, is yes. But only if you know what to do with those ten minutes.

By the end of this chapter, you should be able to:

1. Describe the structural forces that compress behavior-change conversations in modern clinical practice.
2. Summarize the evidence supporting the effectiveness of brief motivational interviewing interventions.
3. Identify the target audiences for this book and their distinct needs.
4. Articulate the core promise of the 10-minute MI framework.

1.1 The Time Famine in Modern Healthcare

The average primary care visit in the United States lasts between 15 and 20 minutes (Tai-Seale et al., 2007). Within that window, the clinician must review the patient's medical history, address the presenting complaint, conduct any necessary physical examination, manage medications, order labs or referrals, document the visit in the electronic health record, and, somewhere in the middle of all of that, attempt to address the lifestyle behaviors that are likely driving the patient's chronic conditions in the first place.

The math does not work. When researchers have measured the actual time spent on behavior-change counseling during primary care visits, the numbers are striking. A study of over 2,500 outpatient visits found that health behavior counseling occurred in only 34 percent of encounters, and when it did occur, it lasted an average of less than one minute (Pollak et al., 2011). In dental settings, the situation is similar. Oral health behavior discussions are frequently compressed into 60 to 90 seconds at the end of a cleaning or examination. In pharmacy settings, medication counseling at the dispensing counter often lasts under two minutes. Telehealth encounters, which were initially hoped to increase time flexibility, have in many systems defaulted to the same 15-to-20-minute blocks as in-person visits.

These time constraints are not the result of clinician apathy. They are structural. Increasing administrative burden, rising patient panel sizes, documentation requirements driven by electronic health records, and reimbursement models that reward volume over depth have collectively created what can fairly be called a time famine. Clinicians across disciplines report feeling rushed, and many describe the behavior-change portion of their encounters as the first thing to get cut when time runs short (Yarnall et al., 2003).

The consequence of this time famine is not simply that behavior-change conversations happen less often. It is that when they do happen, they tend to follow a predictable and largely ineffective pattern. The clinician identifies a problem ("Your blood sugar is too high"), delivers advice ("You need to eat better and exercise more"), and moves on. This approach, sometimes called the "prescribe and hope" model, feels efficient in the moment. It takes less than a minute. It checks a box in the chart. And it almost never works.

The reason it fails is rooted in a concept that motivational interviewing calls the righting reflex. The righting reflex is the natural human impulse to fix what appears broken. When a clinician sees a patient with an A1C of 9.2 and a sedentary lifestyle, the righting reflex says: tell them what to do. Give them the facts. Explain the risks. Surely, if they just understood the danger, they would change.

But decades of research on health behavior tell a different story. People do not change simply because they are told to. In fact, being told to change often produces the opposite of the intended effect. When a patient hears unsolicited advice, a natural psychological response is to defend the current behavior. This is not defiance. It is a normal expression of autonomy. The patient may nod in the office and then continue exactly as before, not because they lack information, but because the conversation did not engage the part of them that is capable of generating genuine motivation.

The righting reflex, unchecked, damages more than just the specific behavior-change conversation. It erodes trust. When patients feel lectured, they become less likely to disclose honestly about their behaviors at future visits. They begin to experience the clinical encounter as adversarial rather than collaborative. Over time, the relationship itself becomes a barrier to change rather than a vehicle for it.

Consider the contrast. Dr. Hassan has three minutes with Mr. Delgado to discuss his diabetes management. If she uses those three minutes to explain (again) why his A1C is dangerous and what he should be eating, she will activate his righting reflex, generate sustain talk ("I know, but I just can't give up my mother's cooking"), and end the visit exactly where she started. But if she uses those three minutes differently, with a single open-ended question, one good reflection, and a small, patient-generated commitment, she has the potential to move the conversation forward in a way that the advice-giving approach never could.

That is the promise of brief motivational interviewing. Not that it will produce dramatic change in a single visit, but that it will consistently move conversations in the right direction, one brief encounter at a time.

1.2 What the Evidence Says About Brief MI

Motivational interviewing has one of the largest evidence bases of any behavioral intervention in healthcare. Since William Miller's original description of the approach in 1983, thousands of studies have examined MI across populations, settings, and health behaviors. What is particularly relevant for our purposes is the subset of that research focused on brief MI interventions, those delivered in one to three sessions, often lasting 15 minutes or less per session.

Two landmark meta-analyses provide the clearest picture. Rubak and colleagues (2005) conducted a systematic review of 72 randomized controlled trials and found that MI outperformed traditional advice-giving in approximately 80 percent of studies. The effect was present even in brief interventions. Lundahl and colleagues (2010) conducted a larger meta-analysis of 119 studies and reported a mean effect size of d = 0.22 across all outcomes, with effect sizes ranging from 0.18 to 0.33 depending on the target behavior. These are small to moderate effect sizes by conventional standards, but in the context of health behavior change, where even modest improvements in adherence or risk reduction translate into meaningful clinical outcomes at the population level, they represent a substantial impact.

What makes these findings especially relevant is the duration of the interventions studied. In the Lundahl meta-analysis, the majority of included studies used interventions of three sessions or fewer, and many used single-session formats lasting 15 minutes or less (Lundahl et al., 2010). A separate meta-analysis focused specifically on MI in medical care settings found a pooled odds ratio of 1.55 (95% confidence interval: 1.40 to 1.71), indicating that patients who received MI were significantly more likely to achieve positive behavior change compared to those who received standard care or no intervention (Frost et al., 2018). The included interventions ranged from single 15-minute contacts to longer treatment courses, but the majority were brief.

The evidence spans a wide range of health behaviors and clinical settings. Brief MI has demonstrated effectiveness for:

Substance use reduction. MI was originally developed for this population, and the evidence here is strongest. Brief MI interventions in primary care have shown significant reductions in alcohol consumption, particularly among patients identified through screening (Moyer et al., 2002).

Medication adherence. Systematic reviews have found that MI improves medication adherence across chronic conditions including HIV, cardiovascular disease, and diabetes, with a pooled relative risk of 1.17 (Palacio et al., 2016).

Physical activity. MI effectively supports physical activity initiation and maintenance by fostering intrinsic motivation and resolving ambivalence around barriers such as time constraints, low confidence, and lack of social support (Frost et al., 2018).

Dietary change. The evidence is more mixed here, with MI showing stronger effects for relatively simple dietary changes (adding fruits and vegetables) than for complex dietary restructuring (long-term adherence to low-sodium diets). Nonetheless, brief MI consistently outperforms standard dietary advice (Thompson et al., 2011).

Smoking cessation. When combined with pharmacotherapy, even brief MI conversations increase quit rates compared to standard care, particularly in primary care and emergency department settings (Hettema et al., 2005).

Oral health behaviors. Studies in dental settings have found that brief MI improves oral hygiene practices and reduces sugar consumption, with effects maintained at follow-up (Cascaes et al., 2014).

The evidence also addresses a concern that many clinicians raise: can someone who is not a trained therapist deliver MI effectively? The answer is a qualified yes. Studies have shown that non-specialist providers, including nurses, pharmacists, community health workers, and dental hygienists, can learn and deliver brief MI with measurable positive effects, provided they receive adequate training and, ideally, ongoing support (Martins & McNeil, 2009). This is an important finding for the premise of this book, which is that brief MI is a learnable, transferable skill that does not require a psychology degree or years of clinical training.

A note of honesty is warranted here. The evidence for brief MI is not uniformly positive. Some studies, particularly those examining brief MI for drug use (as opposed to alcohol), have found no significant difference between MI and control conditions (Saitz et al., 2014). The quality of MI delivery matters enormously. Studies that measure MI fidelity consistently find that when practitioners do not reach proficiency in core MI skills, the intervention loses its effectiveness (Magill et al., 2018). In other words, brief MI works, but only when it is done well. That is precisely why this book exists: to help you do it well, even when time is short.

> **Teaching Point:** *Effect sizes of 0.18 to 0.22 may sound small in a research abstract, but in clinical practice they translate into meaningful differences. An effect size of 0.20 for medication adherence, applied across a panel of 2,000 patients with chronic conditions, represents hundreds of patients making better use of their medications. At the population level, small effects applied consistently are among the most powerful tools in preventive medicine.*

1.3 Who This Book Is For

This book was written for four overlapping audiences, each of whom arrives at the same problem from a different direction.

The first audience is the MI-curious clinician. You have heard of motivational interviewing. Perhaps it came up in a continuing education lecture, a residency rotation, or a conversation with a colleague. You understand the general idea: instead of telling patients what to do, you help them find their own reasons to change. But you have never received formal MI training, and you are not sure how to translate the concept into something you can actually do during a fifteen-minute visit. You need a starting point that is practical, not theoretical. This book provides that starting point.

The second audience is the trained MI practitioner who needs micro-structures. You have attended an MI workshop, perhaps even a multi-day training. You understand the spirit, the processes, and the core skills. But back in the clinic, where visits are short and interruptions are constant, you find it difficult to deploy what you learned. The elegant demonstrations you saw in training do not map neatly onto the reality of a Tuesday afternoon with fourteen patients before lunch. You need a framework that compresses MI into the time you actually have. This book provides that framework.

The third audience is the health coach or wellness professional. You may work in corporate wellness, community health, lifestyle medicine, or private coaching. Your sessions are longer than a primary care visit, but you still need structure. You know that motivational interviewing is considered a gold-standard communication approach for behavior change, and you want to integrate it into your coaching practice in a systematic, repeatable way. This book shows you how to use the 10-minute template as a building block within longer coaching sessions.

The fourth audience is the clinic manager or team leader. You are responsible for the quality of patient interactions across your practice. You want to build a culture where every member of the care team, from the front desk to the physician, communicates in a way that supports patient autonomy and fosters genuine engagement. You need tools that are simple enough to train broadly, structured enough to maintain consistency, and evidence-based enough to justify the investment. This book provides those tools.

Regardless of which audience you belong to, the common thread is this: you believe that conversations about health behavior matter, and you are looking for a way to have those conversations more effectively within the time you actually have.

1.4 The Quick-Start Promise

Here is what this book will give you.

First, a repeatable 10-minute framework. Chapter 5 introduces the Brief MI Template, a structured approach that maps MI's four processes (Engaging, Focusing, Evoking, Planning) onto a clock-based framework. The template is not a script. It is a scaffold. It tells you what to do in each phase, approximately how long each phase should take, and how to transition smoothly from one phase to the next. Once you have practiced it a dozen times, it will become second nature.

Second, a library of ready-to-use questions and phrases. Throughout this book, you will find "Starter Phrases" boxes, "Say This / Not That" comparisons, and pre-built scripts for common clinical scenarios. These are not theoretical examples. They are field-tested language patterns that you can use verbatim until you develop your own voice.

Third, printable tools. The appendices contain everything you need to support your daily practice: the One-Page Consult Sheet, the OARS Quick-Reference Card, Change Talk recognition guides, clinical scenario banks for practice, and self-assessment scorecards. These tools are designed to be photocopied, laminated, and used.

Fourth, a path to continued growth. Chapters 12 through 14 (in Parts Three and Four) provide a self-directed learning plan, guidance for building an MI-consistent team culture, and strategies for sustaining your practice over time. Brief MI is a skill, and like any skill, it improves with deliberate practice and deteriorates without it.

The promise is simple. If you read this book and practice its framework, you will be able to conduct a meaningful, evidence-based, motivational conversation in ten minutes or less, consistently, in any clinical or coaching setting. You will not become an MI expert from reading one book. But you will become competent, and competence, applied daily, changes outcomes.

1.5 Chapter Summary

Modern healthcare operates under a time famine that compresses behavior-change conversations into windows so brief that most clinicians default to advice-giving. This approach, driven by the righting reflex, consistently fails to produce lasting change and often damages the therapeutic relationship. Brief motivational interviewing offers an evidence-based alternative. Meta-analyses demonstrate that MI interventions of one to three sessions, many lasting 15 minutes or less, produce small to moderate effect sizes across a range of health behaviors including substance use, medication adherence, physical activity, dietary change, and smoking cessation. The evidence supports the premise that MI can be delivered effectively by non-specialist providers in time-constrained settings.

This book is designed for MI-curious clinicians, trained practitioners seeking micro-structures, health coaches, and clinic leaders. It provides a repeatable 10-minute framework, ready-to-use language, printable clinical tools, and a path to sustained skill development.

The next chapter provides the conceptual foundation you need before picking up the template: a concise, clinician-friendly overview of motivational interviewing itself.

Chapter 2.0: Motivational Interviewing in 20 Pages

Sarah Chen, a nurse practitioner in a community health center, had just completed a two-hour online module on motivational interviewing. She understood the general philosophy. Be collaborative. Ask open-ended questions. Do not argue with patients. But when she walked into her next appointment with a patient who had been missing dialysis sessions, she realized she had no idea what to actually say. The module had given her the "what" of MI but not the "how." She needed a working model, not a philosophy lecture.

This chapter exists to solve Sarah's problem. It provides a concise, practically oriented overview of motivational interviewing: where it came from, what drives it, how it works, and where it fits in the broader landscape of behavior-change theory. This is not a comprehensive treatment of MI theory. For that, readers should consult Miller and Rollnick's Motivational Interviewing: Helping People Change and Grow (2023), now in its fourth edition. What this chapter provides instead is enough conceptual scaffolding for you to pick up the 10-Minute Template in Chapter 5 and use it with understanding, not just obedience.

By the end of this chapter, you should be able to:

1. Describe the historical origins and defining characteristics of motivational interviewing.
2. Explain the four elements of MI spirit (CAPE) and why they matter more than technique.
3. Outline the four processes of MI and how they relate to each other.
4. Describe the Transtheoretical Model (Stages of Change) and how MI adapts to each stage.
5. Identify and correct common misconceptions about what MI is and is not.

2.1 Where MI Came From

Motivational interviewing was born from a failure. In 1982, William R. Miller, a clinical psychologist working in addiction treatment, was supervising trainee counselors in Norway. As he listened to their recorded sessions and discussed clinical decision-making, he began to articulate something that had been developing in his thinking for years: the confrontational, advice-driven approach that dominated addiction treatment at the time was not just ineffective for many patients. It was actively counterproductive.

The prevailing model in addiction treatment during the 1970s and early 1980s was confrontational. Therapists were trained to break through the patient's "denial" by presenting evidence of the problem forcefully, sometimes aggressively. The assumption was that patients who denied having a problem were psychologically defending against a truth they could not face, and the therapist's job was to dismantle that defense. If a patient resisted the therapist's assessment, the resistance itself was treated as further evidence of the problem.

Miller observed that this approach reliably produced one thing: more resistance. The harder the therapist pushed, the harder the patient pushed back. This was not because patients were pathologically defensive. It was because they were human. When people feel their autonomy is threatened, they defend it. When someone tells them they must change, a natural response is to articulate reasons for staying the same. Miller realized that the confrontational approach was not overcoming resistance. It was creating it.

From this insight, Miller began to describe an alternative approach, one that was collaborative rather than confrontational, that explored ambivalence rather than attacking it, and that drew motivation from the patient rather than imposing it from outside. He published the first formal description of motivational interviewing in 1983 in the journal Behavioural Psychotherapy (Miller, 1983). Stephen Rollnick joined him as a collaborator shortly thereafter, and together they refined and expanded the approach through three subsequent editions of their foundational text, with the most recent published in 2023.

The definition of MI has evolved over the years as the method has been refined, but its current formulation is precise: motivational interviewing is "a collaborative conversation style for strengthening a person's own motivation and commitment to change" (Miller & Rollnick, 2013, p. 12). Each word in that definition matters. "Collaborative" means the clinician works with the patient, not on the patient. "Conversation style" means MI is a way of communicating, not a set of tricks or techniques. "Strengthening a person's own motivation" means the clinician draws out what is already inside the patient rather than installing something new. "Commitment to change" means MI aims not just at awareness or desire but at the decision to act.

Since 1983, MI has expanded far beyond addiction treatment. It is now used in primary care, mental health, criminal justice, education, dental care, pharmacy, public health, coaching, and organizational management. The Motivational Interviewing Network of Trainers (MINT), the international professional body for MI trainers, has members in over 40 countries. MI is recommended by the United States Preventive Services Task Force as a behavioral counseling approach across multiple chronic disease guidelines (Miller & Rollnick, 2013).

The expansion of MI beyond its original context is not simply a matter of marketing. It reflects a core insight that transcends any single population: when people are ambivalent about change, the way you talk with them about that ambivalence determines whether they move toward change or away from it. That insight applies just as powerfully to a patient considering a statin as it does to a person considering sobriety.

2.2 The Spirit of MI: CAPE

If you learn every technique in this book but miss the spirit of MI, you will not be doing motivational interviewing. You will be doing something that looks like MI on the surface but lacks the relational quality that makes it work.

The spirit of MI is the foundational attitude, the "heartset," that underlies every skill and strategy. Miller and Rollnick describe it using four interlocking elements, sometimes remembered with the acronym CAPE: Compassion, Acceptance, Partnership, and Evocation (or Empowerment).

Compassion means that the clinician's primary orientation is toward the patient's welfare. This may sound obvious, but in practice, many clinical conversations are shaped by other priorities: the clinician's agenda, the organization's targets, the insurance company's requirements. Compassion in MI means that the patient's best interests are the organizing principle of the conversation. It does not mean being soft or avoiding difficult truths. It means that when difficult truths are shared, they are shared because they serve the patient, not because they serve the clinician's need to be right.

Acceptance has four components. The first is absolute worth: recognizing the inherent value of every person, regardless of their behavior. The second is accurate empathy: making a genuine effort to understand the patient's perspective, even when you disagree with it. The third is autonomy support: recognizing that the patient has the right to make their own choices, including choices you consider harmful. The fourth is affirmation: actively noticing and naming the patient's strengths, efforts, and values. Acceptance does not mean approval. You can accept a patient fully while being honest about the health consequences of their behavior. What acceptance means is that the patient never feels judged, dismissed, or diminished in your presence.

Partnership means that MI is done "with" someone, not "to" or "for" them. The clinician is not the expert dispensing wisdom to a passive recipient. The patient is the expert on their own life, their own values, and their own barriers. The clinician brings clinical knowledge and conversational skill. Together, they explore the territory of change. This partnership is not a polite fiction. It shapes the entire structure of the conversation. In a partnership-based encounter, the clinician asks more than they tell. They explore more than they direct. They follow the patient's lead even when they have a clear clinical opinion about what the patient should do.

Evocation (or Empowerment) is the element that makes MI fundamentally different from traditional health education. Instead of providing motivation from outside (through information, fear, persuasion, or incentives), MI draws motivation from inside the patient. The underlying assumption is that patients already have within them the values, goals, and concerns that can drive change. The clinician's job is to evoke those internal resources, to help the patient articulate their own reasons for change in their own words. This is not passivity. It is a highly active, strategic form of conversation that requires skill, attention, and discipline.

The distinction between "doing MI" and "being MI-consistent" is worth understanding. Doing MI means deploying specific techniques: open-ended questions, reflections, summaries, change talk reinforcement. Being MI-consistent means embodying the spirit of CAPE in your clinical relationships. A clinician who asks open-ended questions but does so with a judgmental tone is doing MI techniques without MI spirit. A clinician who asks few questions but listens deeply, affirms genuinely, and respects autonomy may be more MI-consistent than the textbook-perfect technique user. The techniques work best when they grow from the spirit. When spirit and technique align, the conversation becomes something greater than the sum of its parts.

> **Teaching Point:** *One useful self-check after any encounter is to ask yourself: "Did I treat that person as a partner or a project?" If the honest answer is "a project," the spirit was missing, regardless of how skillfully you deployed the techniques.*

2.3 The Four Processes of MI

Motivational interviewing unfolds through four overlapping processes: Engaging, Focusing, Evoking, and Planning. These are not rigid sequential steps. They are dynamic, recursive, and sometimes simultaneous. You may engage throughout the conversation. You may return to focusing after a planning discussion reveals uncertainty. You may evoke motivation at any point. The four processes are best understood as layers, each building on the one before, but all potentially active at any given moment.

Engaging is the foundation. It is the process of establishing a mutually trusting and respectful working relationship. Without engagement, nothing else in MI works. Engagement begins before you speak your first clinical word. It begins with how you greet the patient, whether you make eye contact, whether you sit at the same level, whether your body language communicates genuine interest or rushed obligation. Engagement deepens through the use of OARS skills (covered in depth in Chapter 3): open-ended questions that invite the patient to share their story, affirmations that recognize their strengths, reflective listening that demonstrates you are truly hearing them, and summaries that show you have been paying attention.

The tasks of the engaging process include building rapport, reducing defensiveness, and establishing the kind of relationship in which honest conversation about difficult topics becomes possible. A patient who does not feel safe will not tell you the truth about their drinking. A patient who feels judged will not disclose that they stopped taking their medication. Engagement is not a box to check in the first 30 seconds. It is the relational context that must be maintained throughout the entire encounter.

Focusing is the process of developing and maintaining a specific direction in the conversation. MI is not aimless empathic listening. It is a guided conversation with a purpose: to help the patient explore and resolve ambivalence about a specific behavior change. Focusing involves identifying what that specific behavior is.

In some encounters, the focus is obvious. The patient's A1C is 9.2, and the conversation is about diabetes self-management. But in many encounters, the focus is less clear. The patient may have multiple health concerns. The clinician may have a different priority than the patient. The patient may not have identified any desire to change at all. Focusing involves negotiating a shared agenda. It may involve presenting a clinical concern and asking permission to discuss it. It may involve using an "agenda map" to let the patient choose among several possible topics. The goal is to arrive at a single, specific behavior that will be the focus of the evoking and planning processes.

Evoking is the heart of MI and the process that most distinguishes it from other counseling approaches. Evoking is the strategic, skillful process of drawing out the patient's own motivations for change. It involves eliciting "change talk," language in which the patient expresses desire, ability, reasons, need, commitment, activation, or steps toward change. It also involves recognizing and strategically responding to "sustain talk," language in which the patient argues for the status quo. (Chapter 4 covers change talk and sustain talk in detail.)

Evoking is not passive. It is not simply waiting for the patient to express motivation. It involves asking evocative questions ("What would be different in your life if you made this change?"), using the importance and confidence rulers ("On a scale of 0 to 10, how important is it to you to address this?"), reflecting change talk when it appears, and offering double-sided summaries that capture both sides of the patient's ambivalence.

The research on MI process has demonstrated that the amount and strength of change talk during a session predicts subsequent behavior change (Moyers et al., 2007). Equally important, the amount of sustain talk predicts a lack of change. The clinician's behavior directly influences this balance. When clinicians use MI-consistent strategies (open questions, reflections, affirmations), change talk increases. When clinicians use MI-inconsistent strategies (confronting, directing, warning), sustain talk increases. This is not a subtle finding. It means that how you conduct the conversation literally shapes whether the patient moves toward or away from change.

Planning is the process of supporting the patient in developing a concrete plan for change when they are ready. Planning in MI is not the same as prescribing a treatment plan. It is a collaborative process in which the clinician helps the patient articulate what they are willing to do, when they are willing to do it, and how confident they feel about doing it. Planning includes negotiating a specific, achievable commitment (what this book calls a "micro-commitment"), checking the patient's confidence, troubleshooting anticipated barriers, and affirming the patient's autonomy and capability.

Planning is optional in MI. Not every conversation will reach the planning process, and that is perfectly acceptable. If the patient is still deeply ambivalent, pushing toward a plan will feel premature and may generate discord. In such cases, the conversation may end with engagement and evoking, and the plan may emerge in a subsequent visit. Respecting the patient's readiness is not a failure of the method. It is the method working correctly.

2.4 Stages of Change and Where MI Fits

The Transtheoretical Model of behavior change, developed by James Prochaska and Carlo DiClemente in the early 1980s, describes five stages through which people typically move when changing a behavior. Although MI and the Stages of Change model emerged independently and around the same time, they complement each other naturally. Understanding where a patient is in the change process helps the clinician calibrate their MI approach for maximum effectiveness.

The five stages are as follows.

Precontemplation is the stage in which the person is not currently considering change. They may be unaware of the problem, or they may be aware but see no reason to change. They are not "in denial" in a pathological sense. They simply have not yet experienced sufficient motivation, dissonance, or new information to move them toward considering change. In clinical settings, many patients in precontemplation are there because someone else thinks they should change, not because they do. For instance, a patient whose spouse insisted they come to discuss their drinking, but who sees their drinking as perfectly fine, is likely in precontemplation.

Contemplation is the stage in which the person is aware that a problem exists and is seriously thinking about addressing it, but has not yet committed to taking action. This is the stage of ambivalence, the simultaneous experience of wanting to change and wanting to stay the same. Contemplation can last for long periods. A person who has been "thinking about quitting smoking" for three years is in contemplation. MI was specifically designed to work with contemplation, to help people explore and resolve their ambivalence rather than remaining stuck in it.

Preparation is the stage in which the person has decided to change and is beginning to plan how. They may be gathering information, setting dates, telling friends, or making small preliminary adjustments. This stage is brief relative to the others, but it is critical. A patient in preparation is ready for the planning process of MI and will benefit from support in developing a specific, achievable action plan.

Action is the stage in which the person is actively modifying their behavior. They are exercising, taking their medication, attending appointments, reducing their drinking. This stage requires sustained effort and support. MI can help during action by reinforcing commitment, affirming progress, and troubleshooting setbacks.

Maintenance is the stage in which the behavior change has been sustained for a significant period (typically six months or more) and the person is working to prevent relapse. MI in this stage focuses on consolidating gains, exploring challenges to maintenance, and affirming the person's accomplishments.

The practical value of the Stages of Change model for MI practitioners is that it provides a quick diagnostic framework. If you can identify which stage a patient is in, even roughly, you can tailor your MI approach accordingly. A patient in precontemplation does not need a change plan. They need a respectful conversation that plants a seed. A patient in contemplation needs help exploring ambivalence. A patient in preparation needs support in creating a specific, achievable plan. A patient in action needs affirmation and troubleshooting.

You do not need a formal assessment instrument to identify the stage. A single question often suffices. For example: "Where are you right now in terms of thinking about changing your [behavior]? Are you not really thinking about it, are you going back and forth, or are you pretty much ready to do something different?" The patient's response, combined with whatever change talk or sustain talk they produce during the conversation, gives you enough information to calibrate your approach.

The following table summarizes the relationship between the Stages of Change and MI strategy:

Stage	Patient Presentation	Primary MI Strategy
Precontemplation	Not considering change. May be unaware or unconcerned.	Build rapport. Raise awareness gently. Respect autonomy. Plant seeds. Do not push for a plan.
Contemplation	Aware of the problem but ambivalent. Argues both sides.	Explore ambivalence. Evoke change talk. Use importance ruler. Reflect both sides.
Preparation	Has decided to change. Asking questions about how.	Support planning. Help develop specific, achievable steps. Build confidence.

Action	Actively changing behavior. Engaging in new patterns.	Affirm efforts. Troubleshoot barriers. Reinforce commitment.
Maintenance	Sustaining change over time. Guarding against relapse.	Consolidate gains. Explore ongoing challenges. Affirm growth.

2.5 What MI Is Not

Misconceptions about MI are common, even among practitioners who have received some training. Clearing these up is important because acting on a misconception often leads to practice that looks like MI but violates its core principles.

MI is not a trick. MI is sometimes described as a way to "get people to change," as though it were a persuasion technique or a compliance tool. This framing is fundamentally at odds with MI's spirit. MI does not manipulate people into making choices they do not want to make. It helps people access and articulate motivations that are already present but may be obscured by ambivalence, habit, or fear. The goal is not compliance. The goal is autonomous, internally motivated change.

MI is not just asking open-ended questions. Open-ended questions are an important MI skill, but they are only one of four core communication tools (the OARS skills covered in Chapter 3). A clinician who asks a string of open-ended questions without reflecting, affirming, or summarizing is conducting an interrogation, not an MI conversation. The balance between questions and reflections is critical. A common training target is a 2:1 ratio of reflections to questions.

MI is not the same as the Stages of Change model. Although MI and the Transtheoretical Model are complementary and are often taught together, they are distinct frameworks developed independently. MI is a communication approach. The Stages of Change model is a theoretical framework describing how people move through the process of change. You can practice MI without reference to the stages, and you can use the stages model without practicing MI. They work well together, but they are not interchangeable.

MI is not incompatible with giving information. One of the most common fears among clinicians learning MI is that it means they can never share clinical expertise or provide medical information. This is incorrect. MI includes a specific structure for sharing information in a way that respects the patient's autonomy: the Elicit-Provide-Elicit (E-P-E) sequence. In E-P-E, the clinician first elicits what the patient already knows or wants to know, then provides information with permission, then elicits the patient's response. This structure ensures that information is offered as a resource, not imposed as a lecture.

MI is not passive. MI's emphasis on listening and following the patient's lead sometimes creates the impression that the clinician is supposed to sit back and wait. This is a misunderstanding. MI is a highly active, directive (in the sense of goal-directed, not authoritarian) approach. The clinician actively steers the conversation toward the topic of change, strategically reflects change talk, selectively amplifies certain patient statements, and guides the conversation toward planning when the time is right. The skill lies in being active without being coercive.

MI does not require a 50-minute session. This misconception is the entire reason this book exists. MI was originally described in the context of therapeutic sessions, but it has been successfully adapted to encounters as brief as five to fifteen minutes. The principles and skills of MI scale. A single well-placed reflection can shift the direction of a three-minute conversation. A ten-minute encounter using the Brief MI Template (Chapter 5) can accomplish what a 30-minute advice-giving session never will.

2.6 Case Study: Dr. Park and the Reluctant Patient

Background

Dr. James Park is an internist at a busy urban clinic. His patient, Ms. Lorraine Fisher, is a 62-year-old woman with hypertension, hyperlipidemia, and early-stage chronic kidney disease. Her last two appointments were focused on adjusting her medications, but her blood pressure has remained elevated. Her pharmacy records show she has filled her antihypertensive prescription only twice in the past six months. Dr. Park has 18 minutes scheduled for this visit.

Presentation

When Dr. Park asks about her medications, Ms. Fisher looks away and says, "I take them when I remember. Honestly, I don't think they do much." Her tone is flat and slightly defensive. She has heard the medication speech before.

Analysis

Ms. Fisher is in the contemplation stage. She is not refusing to discuss medications, but she is ambivalent. Her statement contains sustain talk ("I don't think they do much") and a hint of a barrier ("when I remember"). A traditional response would be to explain (again) why the medications matter and what could happen if she does not take them. This approach would activate the righting reflex and likely produce more sustain talk.

Response Using MI

Dr. Park resists the righting reflex and instead reflects: "It sounds like you're not convinced the medications are making a difference." Ms. Fisher responds: "I mean, I don't feel any different when I take them." Dr. Park follows with an open question: "What would convince you that they were helping?" This shifts the conversation from defense to exploration. Ms. Fisher mentions that she used to check her blood pressure at the pharmacy and noticed it was sometimes lower. Dr. Park uses this as a bridge: "So when you were checking regularly, you could see the connection. What got in the way of keeping that up?" The conversation continues, and within eight minutes, Ms. Fisher has identified a specific barrier (she stopped going to the pharmacy kiosk when her schedule changed) and a specific solution she generated herself (checking her pressure at her daughter's house, where there is a home monitor). Dr. Park closes with a confidence check: "How confident are you, on a 0-to-10 scale, that you'll check your pressure at your daughter's place this week?" She says seven. He affirms her plan and documents the conversation.

Outcome

At her follow-up visit six weeks later, Ms. Fisher reports that she has been checking her blood pressure weekly and has been more consistent with her medication after seeing the numbers respond. Her blood pressure is lower, though not yet at target. The conversation has shifted from adversarial to collaborative.

Teaching Points

- Reflecting sustain talk without arguing against it opened space for the patient to explore her ambivalence.

- The patient generated her own solution, which dramatically increases the likelihood of follow-through compared to a clinician-imposed plan.

- The confidence ruler (she said 7) served as a quick feasibility check and avoided setting a plan the patient was not confident about completing.

- The entire MI portion of the encounter lasted less than eight minutes.

2.7 Chapter Summary

Motivational interviewing is a collaborative conversation style developed by William Miller and Stephen Rollnick, originating in addiction treatment and now applied across healthcare and beyond. Its spirit, captured in the acronym CAPE (Compassion, Acceptance, Partnership, Evocation), is more important than any individual technique. MI unfolds through four overlapping processes: Engaging, Focusing, Evoking, and Planning. It complements the Transtheoretical Model's Stages of Change by providing the communication tools to help people move through those stages.

MI is not a trick, not just open-ended questions, not the same as the stages model, not incompatible with sharing information, not passive, and not limited to long sessions. It is an active, strategic, evidence-based approach to helping people find and act on their own reasons for change.

With this conceptual foundation in place, the next chapter equips you with the specific communication tools you will use every day: the OARS skills.

Chapter 3.0: The OARS Toolkit

Marcus Jefferson, a pharmacist at a large retail chain, had just attended a lunch-and-learn on motivational interviewing. He was enthusiastic. The next patient who came to the counter to pick up a new statin prescription seemed like the perfect opportunity. Marcus asked an open-ended question: "What do you know about this medication?" The patient gave a brief answer. Marcus asked another open-ended question: "How do you feel about starting it?" The patient answered. Marcus asked a third: "What concerns do you have?" The patient answered again, looking slightly uncomfortable. Marcus realized he had been firing questions like a reporter conducting an interview, and the patient was retreating. He had the right tool but the wrong technique. He was all "O" and no "ARS."

This chapter breaks down the four core communication skills of motivational interviewing, known by the acronym OARS: Open-ended questions, Affirmations, Reflective listening, and Summaries. These are not MI-specific inventions. They are foundational communication skills drawn from the person-centered counseling tradition and refined within the MI framework. What makes them powerful in MI is not any single skill in isolation but the way they work together to create a conversation that moves a person toward their own motivation for change.

By the end of this chapter, you should be able to:

1. Distinguish open-ended from closed-ended questions and recognize when each is appropriate.
2. Deliver affirmations that are genuine, specific, and focused on the person rather than the behavior.
3. Use simple, complex, amplified, and double-sided reflections strategically.
4. Construct collecting, linking, and transitional summaries.
5. Integrate all four OARS skills in a brief clinical encounter.

3.1 Open-Ended Questions

An open-ended question is one that cannot be answered with a single word or a brief factual response. It invites the person to think, reflect, and elaborate. By contrast, a closed-ended question can be answered with "yes," "no," or a specific piece of data.

The distinction matters because the type of question you ask determines the type of answer you get. Closed questions produce closed answers. They are efficient for gathering specific information ("When did you last take your medication?" "Do you smoke?"), but they keep the clinician in the driver's seat and the patient in a passive, responsive role. Open questions shift the dynamic. They invite the patient to do the talking, to explore their own thoughts and feelings, and to generate the kind of language that MI practitioners are listening for: change talk.

Starter Phrases for Open-Ended Questions

"What concerns you most about your health right now?"

"How would you like things to be different?"

"What have you already tried?"

"What would it take for you to feel ready to make a change?"

"Tell me about a time when you were able to make a positive change in your life."

"What is the most important thing for you right now?"

Notice that several of these "questions" are actually statements disguised as invitations ("Tell me about..."). This is intentional. The goal is to open space for the patient to speak, regardless of the grammatical form.

A practical guideline for brief encounters: aim to open with one strong open-ended question, and then shift to reflections and summaries. The most common error among clinicians new to MI is asking too many questions in succession without reflecting. Marcus Jefferson's experience at the pharmacy counter illustrates this trap perfectly. A string of open-ended questions, no matter how good each one is individually, begins to feel like an interrogation. The patient starts giving shorter and shorter answers. The conversational energy drops. The clinician works harder. Everyone gets tired.

The antidote is the reflection, which brings us to the most important skill in the OARS toolkit.

Common Trap: The Question Cascade

Clinicians who are new to MI often rely heavily on questions because questions feel active and productive. The result is what MI trainers call the "question-answer trap" or "question cascade": the clinician asks a question, the patient answers, the clinician asks another question, the patient answers again, and the conversation devolves into an interview rather than a dialogue. The remedy is to follow each question with at least one reflection before asking the next question. A useful clinical target is a 2:1 ratio of reflections to questions throughout the encounter.

3.2 Affirmations

An affirmation is a statement that recognizes something positive about the person: a strength, an effort, a value, or a quality. Affirmations differ from praise in an important way. Praise focuses on behavior and often positions the clinician as the evaluator ("Good job taking your medication this week!"). Affirmation focuses on the person and positions the clinician as a witness ("You have shown real determination in managing your health, even when it has been difficult").

The difference is subtle but consequential. Praise can feel condescending, particularly when it comes from someone in a position of authority. It can also create a dynamic in which the patient performs for the clinician's approval rather than acting from internal motivation. Affirmation, by contrast, supports the patient's self-efficacy and autonomy. It says: I see who you are, not just what you did.

The Affirmation Formula: Notice + Name

Effective affirmations follow a two-part structure. First, you notice something specific about the person. Second, you name the quality or value that underlies it.

For example:

Observation: The patient has come to three consecutive appointments despite transportation challenges.

Affirmation: "You have kept showing up even when getting here is not easy. That tells me this matters to you."

Observation: A patient discloses that they have been drinking more than they would like.

Affirmation: "It took courage to be honest with me about that. You clearly value being straightforward."

Observation: A patient reports that they walked twice last week after months of inactivity.

Affirmation: "You found a way to get started even though you weren't sure it would make a difference. That takes initiative."

Notice that in each case, the affirmation names a personal quality (determination, courage, initiative) rather than simply evaluating the behavior ("Good job walking"). This is what makes an affirmation feel genuine rather than patronizing.

Common Trap: The Hollow Affirmation

An affirmation that is not grounded in a specific observation feels empty. "You're doing great" is not an affirmation. It is a social pleasantry that the patient will likely dismiss. Similarly, affirmations that sound scripted or formulaic ("I really appreciate your willingness to engage in this process") can feel patronizing, especially if the patient is not feeling willing at all. The best affirmations are spontaneous, specific, and honest. If you cannot find something genuine to affirm, do not force it. A single authentic affirmation is worth more than a dozen hollow ones.

3.3 Reflective Listening

Reflective listening is the most important skill in motivational interviewing. It is also the most difficult to master. Miller and Rollnick have described reflective listening as the foundation on which all other MI skills rest (Miller & Rollnick, 2013). Without it, open questions become interrogations, affirmations become disconnected pleasantries, and summaries become recitations. With it, every element of the conversation gains depth and direction.

A reflection is a statement, not a question, in which the clinician offers back to the patient what they seem to be saying, thinking, or feeling. The purpose of a reflection is twofold. First, it demonstrates that the clinician is listening, truly hearing what the patient is communicating, which builds trust and engagement. Second, it gives the patient the experience of hearing their own thoughts articulated by someone else, which can deepen their self-understanding and sometimes shift their perspective.

There are four types of reflections commonly used in MI, each with increasing depth and strategic value.

Simple Reflections

A simple reflection repeats or slightly rephrases what the patient said. It adds no new meaning and does not attempt to infer what the patient might be feeling beneath the surface.

Patient: "I've been trying to eat better, but it's hard with my schedule."

Simple reflection: "Your schedule makes it difficult to eat the way you'd like."

Simple reflections are useful for demonstrating attention, maintaining conversational flow, and buying time when you are not yet sure where the conversation is heading. They are low-risk and always appropriate.

Complex Reflections

A complex reflection goes beyond what the patient explicitly said to reflect the underlying meaning, feeling, or implication. It is a guess, offered as a statement, about what the patient might be experiencing beneath the surface.

Patient: "I've been trying to eat better, but it's hard with my schedule."

Complex reflection: "Part of you wants to make healthier choices, and you're frustrated that your daily life keeps getting in the way."

Notice that the complex reflection names an emotion (frustration) and an internal conflict (wanting to change but being blocked) that the patient did not explicitly state. This is what makes it powerful. If the reflection is accurate, the patient feels deeply understood. If it is slightly off, the patient will correct it, which is also useful because the correction provides new information.

Amplified Reflections

An amplified reflection slightly overstates or exaggerates what the patient said, not with sarcasm but with genuine reflection. The purpose is to invite the patient to step back from their own position and argue for the other side.

Patient: "I don't think I need to change my drinking. It's not that bad."

Amplified reflection: "So your drinking really hasn't caused any problems at all."

If the amplification is done well, the natural response is for the patient to moderate: "Well, I wouldn't say no problems at all. Last month there was that incident with my boss..." This is a classic MI move. The patient, in correcting the overstatement, begins to produce change talk. Amplified reflections must be delivered with a completely neutral, genuine tone. Any hint of sarcasm will destroy the effect and create discord.

Double-Sided Reflections

A double-sided reflection captures both sides of the patient's ambivalence in a single statement, typically using the word "and" (not "but," which negates the first half).

Patient: "I know I should quit smoking, but I really enjoy it. It's the only thing that relaxes me."

Double-sided reflection: "Smoking gives you something you value, a way to unwind, and at the same time, part of you recognizes it's affecting your health."

The double-sided reflection validates the patient's experience of ambivalence without arguing for either side. It gives the patient permission to hold both truths simultaneously, which is often the first step toward resolving the tension between them.

A critical practice note: always end the double-sided reflection on the change side. The last thing the patient hears is the part that leans toward change. This is a subtle but important directional cue.

The 2:1 Ratio

A widely cited clinical target in MI training is a 2:1 ratio of reflections to questions. For every question you ask, aim to offer at least two reflections. This ratio ensures that the conversation feels like a dialogue rather than an interview. It also ensures that the clinician is doing the deeper work of understanding and reflecting, not just gathering information. In brief encounters, achieving a strict 2:1 ratio may not always be possible, but even aiming for 1:1 represents a significant shift for most clinicians, who typically ask far more questions than they offer reflections.

3.4 Summaries

A summary is an extended reflection that pulls together multiple things the patient has said. If reflections are individual brush strokes, a summary is the step back to look at the whole painting. Summaries serve several purposes: they demonstrate that the clinician has been listening carefully, they organize the patient's scattered thoughts into a coherent picture, and they can strategically highlight change talk while acknowledging sustain talk.

There are three types of summaries used in MI.

Collecting Summaries

A collecting summary gathers together several things the patient has said during the conversation. It is like a bouquet: you pick the most important statements and arrange them together.

"Let me see if I have this right. You've been feeling more tired lately, and you're wondering if your medication is contributing to that. At the same time, you noticed that when you were walking regularly last spring, you had more energy. You're also worried about your daughter's upcoming surgery and whether you'll have the bandwidth to focus on your own health right now."

A collecting summary shows the patient that you have been paying attention to the full picture, not just the medical facts.

Linking Summaries

A linking summary connects something the patient said now to something they said earlier in the conversation, or even in a previous visit.

"A few minutes ago, you mentioned that your father had a heart attack at 60. And just now, you said you've been thinking more about your own cholesterol numbers. It sounds like your family history is weighing on you."

Linking summaries help patients see connections they may not have noticed themselves. They can also serve as a bridge to evoking change talk by highlighting the relationship between the patient's values and their current behavior.

Transitional Summaries

A transitional summary is used to signal a shift in the conversation, typically from the evoking process to the planning process. It recaps the conversation so far, emphasizes the change talk the patient has produced, and opens the door to next steps.

"So, to bring this together: you've been thinking about your drinking for a while now. You're clear that it's been affecting your sleep and your relationship with your wife. You mentioned that you felt better during that month last year when you cut back. And you're curious about whether you could do that again. Where does that leave you in terms of what you might want to do next?"

The transitional summary is one of the most powerful tools in brief MI because it efficiently collects everything the conversation has produced and hands it back to the patient as fuel for a decision. In a ten-minute encounter, a well-crafted transitional summary at the seven-minute mark can be the bridge that makes the difference between a conversation that goes nowhere and one that ends with a plan.

Template for a 30-Second Transitional Summary

"So here is what I'm hearing. [Two to three key points from the conversation, emphasizing change talk.] [One acknowledgment of the difficulty or ambivalence.] [A forward-looking question: 'Where does that leave you?' or 'What would you like to do with this?']"

3.5 Putting OARS Together in a Brief Encounter

The following annotated transcript shows all four OARS skills deployed during a five-minute exchange between a clinician and a patient who has been referred for elevated blood pressure and inconsistent medication use. Skill labels appear in brackets.

Clinician: Good to see you today, Mr. Tran. What's on your mind about your health lately? [Open-ended question]

Patient: Honestly, not much. I know my blood pressure is high. My wife keeps telling me to take my pills. But I feel fine, so it's hard to take it seriously.

Clinician: You feel healthy, and that makes it hard to understand why the blood pressure numbers matter. [Simple reflection]

Patient: Exactly. I mean, if I felt sick, I'd take them. But I don't feel anything.

Clinician: So the medication doesn't seem connected to anything you're actually experiencing day to day. And at the same time, there's a part of you that takes your wife's concern seriously, because you're here. [Double-sided reflection]

Patient: Yeah. I don't want to worry her. And my father had a stroke. That's in the back of my mind.

Clinician: That's a heavy thing to carry, knowing your father's history and wondering whether you're on the same path. The fact that you're thinking about it tells me you care about being around for your family. [Complex reflection + Affirmation]

Patient: I do. I've got a granddaughter now. She's two. I want to see her grow up.

Clinician: You want to be there for her. [Simple reflection, reflecting change talk]

Patient: I do. I really do.

Clinician: So let me see if I've got this right. You feel fine physically, which makes the medication feel unnecessary. But your father's stroke is in the back of your mind, and you've got a granddaughter you want to watch grow up. Your wife is worried, and some part of you shares that worry. [Transitional summary] Where does that leave you in terms of the blood pressure medication?

Patient: I guess... I should probably give it a real try. Maybe if I took it every day for a month and checked my numbers, I'd see whether it makes a difference.

Clinician: A month-long trial with regular monitoring. That's a concrete plan. How confident are you, on a 0 to 10, that you can take the medication every day for the next month?

Patient: I'd say about a seven.

Clinician: A seven. That's solid. What would make it an eight?

Patient: If I set a reminder on my phone. I forget because I don't have a routine for it.

Clinician: So a phone reminder could be the thing that makes this work. You've already identified the barrier and the fix. That's problem-solving in action. [Affirmation]

This entire exchange took approximately five minutes. The clinician asked two open-ended questions, delivered four reflections (two simple, one complex, one double-sided), offered two affirmations, and provided one transitional summary. The patient moved from "I feel fine" to "I should probably give it a real try" and generated his own plan with a specific implementation strategy. No advice was given. No lectures were delivered. The patient's own motivation, specifically his granddaughter and his family history, did the heavy lifting.

3.6 Chapter Summary

The OARS skills are the fundamental communication tools of motivational interviewing. Open-ended questions create space for the patient to explore. Affirmations recognize strengths and build self-efficacy. Reflective listening, the most critical and most difficult skill, demonstrates understanding and deepens the conversation. Summaries organize, highlight, and transition. When used together in a balanced and intentional way, these four skills create a conversation that moves people toward change without coercion, argument, or unsolicited advice.

The common pitfall for new practitioners is over-relying on questions at the expense of reflections. Aim for a 2:1 reflection-to-question ratio. Use affirmations that are specific and genuine. End double-sided reflections on the change side. Practice the transitional summary as your go-to tool for shifting from exploration to action.

The next chapter examines the language that MI is designed to elicit and reinforce: change talk and sustain talk.

Chapter 4.0: The Language of Change

Keisha Morgan, a behavioral health consultant embedded in a primary care clinic, was conducting a brief follow-up with a patient named David, a 44-year-old truck driver with untreated sleep apnea who had been refusing a CPAP machine for over a year. Midway through the conversation, David said something that made Keisha's ears perk up: "I mean, my wife says I stop breathing at night. I know it scares her. And I've been so tired that I almost fell asleep on the highway last week." Keisha recognized this immediately. David was not just making conversation. He was producing change talk, language that leaned toward change, even though he had not said the words "I want to use the CPAP." If Keisha reflected this language strategically, she could strengthen it. If she ignored it and instead launched into a list of reasons why CPAP was important, she would likely push David right back into sustain talk. The next thirty seconds of the conversation would determine the direction of the next thirty days.

This chapter teaches you to hear what Keisha heard. Understanding the difference between change talk and sustain talk, and knowing how to respond to each, is the engine that makes motivational interviewing work. Research consistently demonstrates that the amount and strength of change talk during a session predicts subsequent behavior change, and that clinician behavior directly influences how much change talk a patient produces (Moyers et al., 2009; Magill et al., 2014). Learning to recognize and respond to these language patterns is not an advanced MI skill. It is a fundamental one.

By the end of this chapter, you should be able to:

1. Define change talk and explain its significance using the DARN-CAT framework.
2. Distinguish between preparatory change talk (DARN) and mobilizing change talk (CAT).
3. Use at least three strategies to elicit change talk in a brief encounter.
4. Define sustain talk and explain why it is a normal part of ambivalence.
5. Respond to sustain talk using at least four MI-consistent techniques.
6. Recognize discord and know how to repair it.

4.1 What Is Change Talk?

Change talk is any patient language that favors movement toward change. It is the patient's own voice arguing for a different future. When a patient says "I know I need to cut back on the drinking" or "I think I could probably manage a short walk most days," they are producing change talk. When they say "I want to be around to see my kids graduate," they are producing change talk even though the statement is not explicitly about a specific behavior. Change talk is any language that expresses desire, ability, reasons, need, commitment, activation, or steps toward change.

Miller and Rollnick organize change talk using the mnemonic DARN-CAT, which captures seven categories arranged into two groups (Miller & Rollnick, 2013).

Preparatory Change Talk (DARN)

Preparatory change talk signals that the person is considering change but has not yet committed to it. It is the language of contemplation.

Desire statements express wanting. "I wish I could get my blood pressure under control." "I'd like to feel better in the mornings." "I want to be healthier for my family."

Ability statements express capability. "I think I could cut back to two cigarettes a day." "I've done it before, so I know I can do it again." "If I really set my mind to it, I could probably manage."

Reason statements express why. "If I don't get my diabetes under control, I could lose my eyesight." "I'd save a lot of money if I quit smoking." "My doctor said the medication would help with the fatigue."

Need statements express urgency or necessity. "I have to do something about this weight." "Something has to change." "I can't keep going like this."

Mobilizing Change Talk (CAT)

Mobilizing change talk is stronger. It signals movement from contemplation toward action.

Commitment statements express intention to act. "I will call the nutritionist this week." "I'm going to start walking." "I've decided to cut back."

Activation statements express readiness without specifying action. "I'm ready to do something about this." "I think the time is right." "I'm willing to give it a try."

Taking steps statements describe actions already taken. "I actually went for a walk yesterday." "I threw away the rest of the pack." "I signed up for that class."

The distinction between DARN and CAT matters clinically. Preparatory change talk is important and should be reinforced, but it does not reliably predict behavior change on its own. Someone can express desire, ability, reasons, and need and still not change. Mobilizing change talk, particularly commitment language, is the strongest predictor of actual change (Amrhein et al., 2003). The practical implication is that your job as a clinician is to help patients move from DARN to CAT: from thinking about change to committing to it and taking action.

4.2 Eliciting Change Talk

Change talk does not always arise spontaneously. Often, the clinician needs to invite it into the conversation through strategic questioning and reflection. The following techniques are among the most effective for eliciting change talk in brief encounters.

Evocative Questions

These are open-ended questions specifically designed to draw out change talk. They invite the patient to articulate their own reasons, desires, and capacities for change.

"What would be different in your life if you made this change?"

"What are the best reasons for doing something about this?"

"How would you like things to be a year from now?"

"What would you be willing to try?"

The Importance Ruler

"On a scale of 0 to 10, where 0 is not at all important and 10 is the most important thing in your life, how important is it to you to [change the behavior]?"

After the patient gives a number, follow with: "Why did you choose that number and not a lower one?"

This question is the key to the ruler technique. By asking why the patient did not say a lower number, you invite them to articulate the reasons they do care, which is change talk. If the patient says 4, asking "Why not a 2?" produces change talk. Asking "Why not a 6?" produces sustain talk. The direction of the follow-up question determines the direction of the conversation.

The Confidence Ruler

"On the same 0-to-10 scale, how confident are you that you could make this change if you decided to?"

The gap between importance and confidence is diagnostically useful. A patient who scores high on importance but low on confidence needs help with barriers, planning, and self-efficacy. A patient who scores low on importance but high on confidence may need more evoking work around values and goals.

Looking Back

"Tell me about a time in the past when you were able to make a significant change. What made that possible?"

This question connects the patient to their own history of success, which strengthens self-efficacy and produces ability change talk.

Looking Forward

"Imagine it's a year from now and things have changed for the better. What does your life look like?"

Future-oriented questions invite the patient to construct a mental image of a changed life, which strengthens desire and reason change talk.

Querying Extremes

"What concerns you most about continuing on the current path?"

"What is the best thing that could happen if you made this change?"

These questions push the patient to the edges of their ambivalence, where change talk tends to be strongest.

4.3 What Is Sustain Talk?

Sustain talk is any patient language that favors the status quo. It is the other side of ambivalence: the voice that says "I don't want to change," "I can't change," "There's no reason to change," or "I don't need to change." Sustain talk mirrors the DARN categories in reverse: desire to stay the same, inability to change, reasons against change, and no perceived need for change.

Understanding sustain talk requires letting go of the concept of "resistance." In earlier models of behavior change, when a patient pushed back against the clinician's recommendations, it was labeled resistance and treated as a problem to be overcome. MI reframes this entirely. What was once called resistance is actually a predictable, normal expression of ambivalence. The patient is not being difficult. They are being human. They are experiencing the completely natural pull of the status quo, the comfort of the familiar, the fear of the unknown, the rational assessment that change involves effort, risk, and loss.

The crucial insight from MI research is this: how the clinician responds to sustain talk determines whether it grows or shrinks. When a clinician argues against sustain talk ("But you need to take your medication"), the patient defends it more vigorously. This is not defiance. It is a basic human response to perceived pressure. When a clinician reflects sustain talk without arguing against it, the patient often softens or even spontaneously produces change talk in response. This counterintuitive dynamic is one of the most important findings in MI research and one of the hardest for clinicians to internalize (Miller & Rose, 2009).

4.4 Responding to Sustain Talk Without Fueling It

The following techniques allow you to acknowledge sustain talk, honor the patient's experience, and create space for change talk to emerge, all without arguing, correcting, or lecturing.

Straight Reflection

Simply reflect back what the patient said, without adding or challenging. This shows the patient they have been heard, which paradoxically often reduces the intensity of the sustain talk.

Patient: "I don't think my drinking is that big of a deal."

Clinician: "You see your drinking as pretty manageable."

When the patient hears their own statement reflected back neutrally, they often begin to qualify it: "Well, I mean, there have been a couple of times..."

Amplified Reflection

Slightly overstate the patient's sustain talk, without sarcasm, to invite them to argue against their own position.

Patient: "I really can't give up smoking. It's impossible."

Clinician: "There's absolutely no way you could ever quit, no matter what."

The natural response is to moderate: "I wouldn't say absolutely no way. I did manage to cut down during my pregnancy." The patient has just produced ability change talk without being asked for it.

This technique requires a genuine, empathic tone. If the amplification sounds mocking, it will create discord rather than change talk.

Double-Sided Reflection

Capture both sides of the patient's ambivalence in one statement, always ending on the change side.

Patient: "I know I should exercise, but I just hate it."

Clinician: "You really dislike exercising, and at the same time, you recognize it could make a difference for you."

The "and" is important. Using "but" ("You dislike exercise, but you know it would help") negates the first half and sounds like a correction. Using "and" holds both truths simultaneously, which validates the patient's full experience.

Emphasizing Autonomy

Explicitly affirm the patient's right to make their own choice.

Patient: "I'm not ready to quit drinking."

Clinician: "That's completely your decision. No one can force you to change, and I wouldn't try."

This often produces a paradoxical effect. When patients feel their autonomy is genuinely respected, the pressure to defend the status quo decreases, and they become more open to exploring change.

Reframing

Offer an alternative interpretation of the patient's situation that casts their experience in a new light.

Patient: "I've tried to lose weight a dozen times and I always fail."

Clinician: "You've made a dozen attempts, which tells me this is something you keep coming back to because it matters to you."

The reframe does not deny the patient's experience of failure. It adds a new layer of meaning: persistence as evidence of importance.

Coming Alongside

Align yourself with the sustain talk rather than against it. This is sometimes called "rolling with resistance" in older MI terminology.

Patient: "Honestly, I don't think I need to change anything."

Clinician: "And maybe you don't. You know your life better than anyone. I'm curious, though, what brought you in today?"

Coming alongside reduces defensiveness and creates an opening for exploration.

4.5 Navigating Discord

Discord is different from sustain talk. Sustain talk is about the behavior (the patient argues for the status quo). Discord is about the relationship (the patient is pushing back against the clinician). Signals of discord include arguing ("That's not what I said"), interrupting, disengaging (one-word answers, looking at the phone), and ignoring (changing the subject abruptly).

Discord usually means the clinician has moved too fast, pushed too hard, or made the patient feel judged. It is a signal to adjust, not to push harder. The following strategies can repair discord:

Reflect the emotion: "I can see this conversation is frustrating for you."

Apologize: "I may have come at this in a way that didn't feel right. That's on me."

Emphasize autonomy: "I'm not trying to push you in any direction. This is your call."

Shift back to engagement: "Let me step back. What's most important to you right now?"

Discord is not a failure. It is feedback. When handled well, it can actually deepen the therapeutic relationship because the patient learns that the clinician can hear negative feedback and respond with respect rather than defensiveness.

4.6 Case Study: Keisha and David Revisited

Background

David, the 44-year-old truck driver introduced at the start of this chapter, has been refusing CPAP therapy for over a year despite severe obstructive sleep apnea. His wife is frightened by his episodes of apnea during sleep. He recently had a near-miss falling asleep at the wheel.

Presentation

David's sustain talk is dominant early in the conversation: "That mask is ridiculous. I'm not sleeping with a machine strapped to my face." But interspersed with the sustain talk are flickers of change talk: "My wife says I stop breathing" (Reason), "I've been so tired I almost fell asleep on the highway" (Reason/Need), and, later, "I guess I'd try it if there was something less annoying than that mask" (Ability, conditional).

Analysis Using DARN-CAT

David has produced Reason change talk (wife's fear, near-miss on the highway) and conditional Ability change talk ("I'd try it if..."). He has not yet produced Desire, Commitment, or Activation change talk. He is in the contemplation stage, leaning toward change but not yet ready to commit.

Response

Keisha reflects the change talk strategically: "The near-miss on the highway shook you. And knowing your wife is scared when she hears you stop breathing at night, that weighs on you too." She follows with an evocative question: "What matters most to you when you think about all this?" David says: "Being safe on the road. I've got to keep my CDL." Keisha reflects: "Your livelihood depends on staying alert, and right now, that's being threatened." David nods.

Keisha does not push for CPAP. Instead, she uses E-P-E: "Would it be helpful if I shared some information about the different options available now? The technology has changed a lot." David agrees. She briefly describes newer mask designs and oral appliances, then closes the loop: "What stands out to you from what I just shared?" David expresses interest in the oral appliance. Keisha closes with a micro-commitment: "Would you be willing to schedule a consultation with the sleep specialist to learn more about that option?" David says yes.

Outcome

David followed through on the consultation and began using an oral appliance. His adherence has been inconsistent, but his near-miss episodes have stopped, and his wife reports improved sleep quality. The conversation is ongoing.

Teaching Points

- Change talk can appear as small fragments embedded in sustain talk. Listening for it requires active attention.

- Reflecting change talk selectively strengthens it. Keisha did not argue against the sustain talk about the mask. She acknowledged it and moved toward the change talk.

- The patient generated his own motivation (safety, CDL, wife's fear). Keisha evoked it. She did not install it.

- E-P-E allowed Keisha to share information without lecturing, and it led the patient to a self-selected next step.

4.7 Chapter Summary

Change talk and sustain talk are the raw materials of motivational interviewing. Change talk, organized by the DARN-CAT framework, encompasses preparatory language (Desire, Ability, Reason, Need) and mobilizing language (Commitment, Activation, Taking steps). The amount and strength of change talk predicts actual behavior change. Clinicians can elicit change talk through evocative questions, importance and confidence rulers, looking back and forward, and querying extremes.

Sustain talk is a normal expression of ambivalence, not a pathology to be defeated. Responding to sustain talk with straight reflection, amplified reflection, double-sided reflection, autonomy emphasis, reframing, or coming alongside can reduce its intensity and create space for change talk to emerge. Discord signals a relationship strain and calls for repair through empathy, apology, and a return to engagement.

With the foundations of MI now in place, including its history, spirit, core skills, and the language of change, we are ready for the centerpiece of this book: the 10-Minute MI Template.

PART TWO: THE 10-MINUTE FRAMEWORK

Chapter 5.0: The Brief MI Template: Open, Focus, Evoke, Plan

Dr. Tanya Okafor had twelve minutes. Her patient, Mrs. Gloria Reyes, was a 67-year-old woman with type 2 diabetes, mild depression, and a recent fall that had made her afraid to leave the house. Her A1C was 8.9. Her most recent PHQ-9 score was 12. She had not been to her podiatrist in eight months. The electronic health record displayed a care plan with six outstanding action items. Dr. Okafor knew she could not address everything. She also knew that if she tried to address everything, she would address nothing well. She needed a structure that would allow her to have one meaningful conversation about one thing that mattered to Mrs. Reyes, in the time she actually had. She needed the 10-Minute MI Template.

This chapter introduces the framework that is the centerpiece of this book. The template maps the four MI processes, Engaging, Focusing, Evoking, and Planning, onto a practical, clock-based structure that fits within a ten-minute window. It is not a script. Scripts are rigid, impersonal, and fall apart in real encounters. It is a scaffold: a flexible structure that provides direction and timing while leaving room for the clinician to respond to whatever the patient brings into the room.

By the end of this chapter, you should be able to:

1. Describe the four phases of the 10-Minute MI Template and the approximate time allocation for each.
2. Identify appropriate opening questions for the OPEN phase.
3. Use the Elicit-Provide-Elicit strategy to share clinical information during the FOCUS phase.
4. Deploy at least two change talk elicitation techniques during the EVOKE phase.
5. Negotiate a micro-commitment during the PLAN phase and check confidence.
6. Adapt the template to a 5-minute "Express MI" format when time is extremely limited.

5.1 The Template at a Glance

The 10-Minute MI Template divides a brief encounter into four phases, each aligned with one of MI's four processes.

Minutes 0 to 2: OPEN (Engage and Agenda Set)

The first two minutes establish the relational foundation and identify what the conversation will be about. This phase uses the Engaging process and the beginning of the Focusing process.

Minutes 2 to 4: FOCUS (Identify the Target Behavior)

The next two minutes narrow the conversation to a single, specific, actionable behavior. This phase completes the Focusing process and may involve sharing clinical information using the Elicit-Provide-Elicit structure.

Minutes 4 to 7: EVOKE (Elicit and Reinforce Change Talk)

The middle three minutes are the heart of the encounter. This phase uses the Evoking process to draw out the patient's own motivations for change, using evocative questions, rulers, and strategic reflections.

Minutes 7 to 10: PLAN (Negotiate a Micro-Commitment)

The final three minutes translate the patient's motivation into a concrete, achievable next step. This phase uses the Planning process to negotiate a micro-commitment, check confidence, troubleshoot barriers, and close with a summary and affirmation.

These time allocations are approximate. Some encounters will spend more time in OPEN (a patient who arrives distressed needs extra engagement time). Some will compress FOCUS into thirty seconds (the target behavior is already obvious). Some will cycle back to EVOKE after a planning discussion reveals unexpected ambivalence. The template is a rhythm, not a metronome. Learn the rhythm, and then adapt it to the music of each encounter.

5.2 Minutes 0 to 2: OPEN

The OPEN phase has two jobs: establish a collaborative tone and set the agenda.

Establishing the Collaborative Tone

The first words out of your mouth set the emotional temperature for the entire encounter. If you begin by reviewing lab values ("Your A1C is up again"), you have immediately positioned yourself as the evaluator and the patient as the subject. If you begin with a directive ("We need to talk about your diet"), you have activated the righting reflex before the patient has spoken a word. If you begin with an open-ended, patient-centered question, you signal that this is a conversation between two people, not a lecture from one to another.

Three proven openers for the OPEN phase:

"What matters most to you about your health right now?"

"How are things going since we last talked?"

"What's been on your mind lately when it comes to your health?"

Each of these invitations gives the patient permission to set the starting point. They may raise the very issue you planned to discuss. They may raise something entirely different. Either way, you now know what is most alive for them, which is the best possible foundation for a productive conversation.

Setting the Agenda

In many encounters, there is more than one potential topic. The patient may have multiple chronic conditions, several overdue preventive measures, and a new concern that emerged since the last visit. The clinician may have a specific agenda based on lab results or a quality measure. When these agendas compete, the first instinct is for the clinician to prioritize based on clinical urgency. This is understandable but often counterproductive. If the patient is worried about their upcoming surgery and you insist on talking about their A1C, you will have a distracted, disengaged conversation partner.

The agenda-setting technique allows you to honor both agendas without forcing one over the other.

"I noticed your A1C has come up a bit, and I'd like to talk about that if you're open to it. I also want to hear what's on your mind. Where would you like to start?"

"There are a few things we could talk about today: your blood pressure medication, the exercise plan we discussed last time, and whatever else is on your mind. Which feels most important to you right now?"

When the patient chooses the focus, their engagement increases. They are invested in the conversation because it is about something they selected. And the topics they did not choose are not lost. They are parked: "Let's make sure we come back to the blood pressure at your next visit."

The Permission Question

When you need to raise a topic the patient has not mentioned, ask permission before proceeding.

"I've been thinking about your lab results. Would it be OK if we spent a few minutes talking about what they mean?"

"I noticed you haven't filled your blood pressure prescription in a while. Would you be comfortable if we explored that a bit?"

The permission question is not a formality. It is a genuine expression of Partnership and Autonomy, two pillars of MI spirit. When you ask permission and the patient grants it, you have a collaborative starting point. When the patient declines, you have important information about their readiness, and you have preserved the relationship for future conversations.

5.3 Minutes 2 to 4: FOCUS

The FOCUS phase narrows the conversation to one specific, actionable behavior. This is where many clinicians get stuck, because the temptation is to try to cover everything. Resist that temptation. One behavior, addressed well, in a single encounter, is worth more than five behaviors mentioned in passing.

Narrowing to One Behavior

The patient's response to the OPEN phase usually provides enough direction to identify a focus. If the patient said "I've been thinking about my drinking," the focus is clear. If the patient said "I just feel tired all the time," the focus requires more exploration: is the fatigue related to sleep, medication side effects, depression, inactivity, or something else? A follow-up question can help: "What do you think is behind the tiredness?"

Once a behavior is identified, state it clearly and check that the patient agrees it is worth discussing.

"So it sounds like the main thing today is the difficulty you've been having with the CPAP. Is that right?"

"It seems like the exercise has been on your mind. Would that be a good thing for us to focus on today?"

The Elicit-Provide-Elicit Strategy

When you need to share clinical information during the FOCUS phase (lab results, screening scores, treatment options), use the Elicit-Provide-Elicit (E-P-E) structure. This is the MI-consistent way to give information without lecturing.

Step 1: Elicit what the patient already knows or wants to know.

"What do you already know about what an A1C number means?"

"What have you heard about the connection between sleep apnea and driving safety?"

Step 2: Provide information, briefly and with permission.

"Would it be helpful if I shared what the latest research says about this?"

Then share the information in two to three sentences. No more. Brevity is critical.

Step 3: Elicit the patient's response.

"What do you make of that?"

"How does that land for you?"

"What stands out to you from what I just said?"

E-P-E accomplishes two things simultaneously. First, it delivers the clinical information the patient needs. Second, it preserves the patient's sense of autonomy and engagement. The patient is not being lectured at. They are being consulted, informed, and then invited to respond. The third step, the closing elicit, is the most important because it returns the conversation to the patient's perspective and often produces change talk.

Linking to Values

One of the most powerful FOCUS moves is connecting the target behavior to something the patient values. If a patient values independence and their untreated diabetes threatens their ability to live alone, naming that connection can transform a clinical fact into a personal urgency.

"You mentioned earlier that staying in your own home is really important to you. The diabetes is connected to that, isn't it?"

5.4 Minutes 4 to 7: EVOKE

The EVOKE phase is the heart of the template. This is where the clinician's MI skills are most fully deployed and where the conversation either generates momentum toward change or stalls.

Deploying the Rulers

The importance and confidence rulers are efficient, versatile tools for the EVOKE phase.

For importance: "On a scale of 0 to 10, where 0 is not at all important and 10 is the most important thing in your life, how important is it to you to [change behavior]?"

Follow-up: "You said a 6. Why a 6 and not a 3?" (This elicits change talk.)

For confidence: "On the same scale, how confident are you that you could do this if you decided to?"

Follow-up: "What would it take to move you from a 5 to a 7?" (This identifies barriers and elicits problem-solving.)

The rulers are especially valuable in brief encounters because they quickly surface both motivation and barriers in a format that is easy to document and track across visits.

Using Evocative Questions

Deploy at least one strong evocative question during this phase:

"What would be different in your daily life if you made this change?"

"What are the three best reasons for doing something about this?"

"If you could snap your fingers and things were different, what would that look like?"

Reflecting Change Talk

When the patient produces change talk, reflect it. This is the single most important thing you can do in the EVOKE phase. Change talk that is reflected is strengthened. Change talk that is ignored dissipates.

Patient: "I guess if I lost some weight, my knees wouldn't hurt as much when I play with my grandson."

Clinician: "Being able to play with your grandson without pain, that's a powerful reason."

The Double-Sided Summary

Near the end of the EVOKE phase, offer a double-sided summary that captures the patient's ambivalence and ends on the change side.

"So on one hand, changing your diet feels overwhelming, especially with everything else you're managing right now. And on the other hand, you've seen what happens when your blood sugar is better controlled: you feel more energetic, you sleep better, and you can do more with your family. Where does that leave you?"

5.5 Minutes 7 to 10: PLAN

The PLAN phase translates motivation into action. Not all encounters will reach this phase. If the patient is in precontemplation or early contemplation, pushing for a plan is premature. But when the patient has produced mobilizing change talk (commitment, activation, or taking steps), the PLAN phase helps them solidify that momentum into something concrete.

The Micro-Commitment

A micro-commitment is one small, specific, measurable step that the patient is willing to take before the next contact. It is not a comprehensive lifestyle overhaul. It is not a vague aspiration. It is a single, achievable action.

Bad micro-commitment: "I'll try to eat healthier."

Good micro-commitment: "I'll eat a salad for lunch on Monday, Wednesday, and Friday this week."

Bad micro-commitment: "I'll exercise more."

Good micro-commitment: "I'll walk around the block after dinner on Tuesday and Thursday."

The specificity matters. Research on implementation intentions, the "if-then" or "when-then" plans that connect a behavior to a specific time, place, and context, consistently shows that specific plans are far more likely to be carried out than general intentions (Gollwitzer, 1999).

Brief Action Planning Integration

Brief Action Planning (BAP), developed by Steven Cole and colleagues, offers a streamlined structure for the PLAN phase that integrates naturally with the MI template (Cole et al., 2019).

The core BAP question: "Is there anything you'd be willing to do in the next week or two to move in the direction we've been talking about?"

This question is MI-consistent because it uses the patient's own language ("the direction we've been talking about"), emphasizes willingness rather than obligation, and keeps the time frame short and manageable.

The Confidence Check

After the patient identifies a micro-commitment, check their confidence:

"On a 0-to-10 scale, how confident are you that you can [specific commitment] in the next [time frame]?"

If confidence is 7 or above, the plan is likely achievable. Affirm the plan and move to closing.

If confidence is below 7, the plan needs adjustment. Ask: "What would need to change to bring that number up?" or "Would a smaller version of this plan feel more doable?" Scaling down a plan to increase confidence is always better than keeping an ambitious plan that the patient does not believe they can complete.

The Closing Summary and Affirmation

End the encounter with a brief summary of what was discussed and what the patient has committed to, followed by an affirmation.

"So just to recap: you're going to try walking after dinner on Tuesday and Thursday, and you'll check your blood sugar before and after to see if it makes a difference. You came up with that plan yourself, and that tells me you're someone who takes ownership of their health. I'll look forward to hearing how it goes."

The closing affirmation is not throwaway politeness. It is a deliberate reinforcement of the patient's agency and capability. The last thing the patient hears before walking out the door should be something that builds their confidence, not something that reminds them of their deficits.

5.6 What If You Only Have 5 Minutes?

Some encounters will not allow ten minutes for behavior change. An urgent care visit, a pharmacy consultation, or a packed clinic day may compress the available window to five minutes or less. The Express MI variant strips the template to its essentials.

The Express MI Format (5 Minutes)

Minutes 0:00 to 0:30: OPEN

One warm-up sentence and one open-ended question.

"Good to see you. What's most important to you health-wise right now?"

Minutes 0:30 to 1:30: ASK

One strong evocative question.

"On a 0-to-10 scale, how important is it to you to [behavior]? Why that number and not lower?"

Minutes 1:30 to 3:00: REFLECT AND SUMMARIZE

Reflect the change talk produced. Offer a brief double-sided or transitional summary.

"So you're worried about [concern], and you can see that [behavior change] could help with that."

Minutes 3:00 to 4:00: COMMIT

Negotiate one micro-commitment.

"Is there one small thing you'd be willing to try before our next visit?"

Confidence check: "How confident, 0 to 10?"

Minutes 4:00 to 5:00: CLOSE

Affirm the commitment and the person.

"You've identified something concrete, and that takes initiative. Let's check in on how it goes."

The Express MI format sacrifices depth for structure. It will not resolve deep ambivalence or address complex psychosocial barriers. What it will do is plant a seed, move the conversation forward by even one step, and preserve the relationship for future encounters. In the landscape of brief clinical interactions, that is often enough.

5.7 Case Study: Dr. Okafor and Mrs. Reyes

Background

Dr. Tanya Okafor has twelve minutes with Mrs. Gloria Reyes, a 67-year-old woman with type 2 diabetes, mild depression, and recent fall-related anxiety. Her A1C is 8.9 and her PHQ-9 score is 12. Six items on the care plan are overdue.

Applying the Template

OPEN (Minutes 0 to 2):

Dr. Okafor begins: "Mrs. Reyes, I'm glad to see you. There are a few things we could talk about today, but I want to start with you. What's been weighing on you the most lately?"

Mrs. Reyes says: "Honestly, it's the fall. I'm scared it's going to happen again. I don't go outside anymore unless my daughter takes me."

Dr. Okafor reflects: "The fall really shook your confidence. You went from getting around on your own to feeling like you need someone with you to be safe."

FOCUS (Minutes 2 to 4):

The fall and associated immobility are connected to multiple items on the care plan (diabetes management, depression, podiatry). Dr. Okafor selects mobility as the focus, since it is what the patient raised and it intersects with several clinical concerns.

"It sounds like getting your confidence back around walking is the thing that would make the biggest difference right now. Would it be OK if we talked about that?"

Mrs. Reyes agrees. Dr. Okafor uses E-P-E: "What have you tried so far to feel safer?" (Elicit). Mrs. Reyes mentions a cane her daughter bought. Dr. Okafor shares that physical therapy can help rebuild balance and confidence after a fall (Provide). "What do you think about that idea?" (Elicit). Mrs. Reyes expresses cautious interest.

EVOKE (Minutes 4 to 7):

"On a 0-to-10 scale, how important is it to you to be able to get around on your own again?"

"A 9."

"A 9. What makes it so high?"

"I've always been independent. I raised four kids by myself. I can't stand depending on anyone."

Dr. Okafor reflects the change talk: "Independence is a core part of who you are, and losing it to this fall feels like losing part of yourself."

Mrs. Reyes tears up: "That's exactly what it feels like."

PLAN (Minutes 7 to 10):

"You mentioned the physical therapy idea resonated with you. Would you be willing to schedule an initial appointment with our PT team?"

"Yes. I think so."

"How confident are you, 0 to 10, that you'll make that call this week?"

"Maybe a 6."

"A 6. What would make it a 7?"

"If someone could call me with the number. I get confused with the phone system here."

Dr. Okafor arranges for the medical assistant to call Mrs. Reyes with the PT number and helps her set a date. She closes: "Mrs. Reyes, the fact that you're ready to take this step tells me the woman who raised four kids on her own is still very much here. I'll check in next visit to see how it's going."

Outcome

Mrs. Reyes attended three physical therapy sessions over the following month. Her mobility improved and she began walking to the mailbox independently. Her PHQ-9 score at the next visit was 9, down from 12. Her A1C was not discussed during this visit. It will be addressed at the next one, building on the momentum of this success.

Teaching Points

- Addressing the patient's stated concern (the fall) rather than the clinician's priority (A1C) produced greater engagement and a concrete outcome.

- The independence value ("I raised four kids by myself") was the emotional engine of the change. Evoking it was the turning point of the encounter.

- A confidence score of 6 prompted troubleshooting, which identified a specific, fixable barrier (phone system confusion). Without the confidence check, this barrier would have silently prevented follow-through.

- The total behavior-change portion of the encounter lasted approximately ten minutes.

5.8 Chapter Summary

The 10-Minute MI Template provides a practical, clock-based structure for conducting brief MI encounters. Its four phases, OPEN, FOCUS, EVOKE, and PLAN, align with MI's four processes and allocate time in proportions that reflect clinical priorities: enough time for engagement and evoking, enough time for a concrete plan, and enough flexibility to adapt when encounters do not follow the expected script. The Express MI variant compresses the framework to five minutes for ultra-brief encounters.

The template's signature tools are the permission question (OPEN), the Elicit-Provide-Elicit structure (FOCUS), the importance and confidence rulers (EVOKE), the micro-commitment with confidence check (PLAN), and the closing affirmation. Together, these tools ensure that every minute of the encounter is used with intention.

The next chapter deepens your skill in each of these tools, with detailed guidance, common errors, and "Say This / Not That" comparisons.

Chapter 6.0: Mastering the Micro-Skills

Rafael Estrada, a physician assistant in a family medicine practice, had been using the 10-Minute MI Template for three weeks. The structure felt helpful, but something was off. His EVOKE phase kept stalling. Patients would give him a number on the importance ruler, and then he would not know what to do next. His reflections felt flat. His plans felt vague. He knew the template, but he had not yet mastered the micro-skills that make each phase work. The template was the skeleton. He needed the muscle.

This chapter provides that muscle. It takes each of the template's key techniques, Elicit-Provide-Elicit, reflective listening under time pressure, the rulers, menu of options, and the micro-commitment, and examines them at the granular level. For each skill, you will find detailed guidance, common errors with corrections, and "Say This / Not That" comparisons that you can practice and internalize.

By the end of this chapter, you should be able to:

1. Execute the Elicit-Provide-Elicit sequence smoothly in under two minutes.
2. Deliver a meaningful reflection in a single sentence, even under time pressure.
3. Use the importance and confidence rulers diagnostically, not just as conversation starters.
4. Present a menu of options that preserves patient autonomy.
5. Help a patient construct a micro-commitment that is specific, achievable, and genuinely their own.

6.1 The Elicit-Provide-Elicit Deep Dive

The Elicit-Provide-Elicit (E-P-E) sequence is MI's answer to the most common challenge in clinical communication: how do you share important medical information without turning into a lecturer?

Why E-P-E Matters More in Brief Encounters

In a fifty-minute therapy session, there is time to recover from a poorly received piece of advice. In a ten-minute encounter, there is not. When a clinician launches into an explanation of why the patient's cholesterol numbers are dangerous, the patient's internal response is often some version of "Here we go again." The righting reflex activates. The patient becomes passive. The conversation loses energy. And the clinician, sensing disengagement, talks faster and more emphatically, which makes the problem worse.

E-P-E prevents this spiral by bookending the information with the patient's own voice.

Step 1: Elicit

Open by exploring what the patient already knows, believes, or wants to know.

"What do you already know about how blood pressure affects the kidneys?"

"What have you heard about this medication?"

"What would you like to know about your test results?"

This first step accomplishes several things. It tells you where the patient is starting from (you may be surprised by how much or how little they know). It engages the patient's brain in active processing rather than passive reception. And it communicates respect: you are not assuming ignorance.

Step 2: Provide

Share the information briefly and with explicit permission.

"Would it be all right if I shared a few things about what we're seeing in your lab results?"

Then deliver the information in two to three sentences. This is critical. More than three sentences, and you have crossed the line from informing to lecturing. The art of the Provide step is compression: saying only what is most essential and saying it clearly.

Say This: "Your A1C of 8.9 means your average blood sugar over the past three months has been higher than the target range. Over time, that can affect your eyes, kidneys, and nerves."

Not That: "So, your A1C is 8.9, which, as you may know, represents the glycated hemoglobin level, which is a measure of your average blood glucose over the past 90 days, and ideally we'd like to see that below 7, though some guidelines say below 6.5, and the reason that matters is that sustained hyperglycemia causes microvascular damage, which can lead to retinopathy, nephropathy, neuropathy, and macrovascular complications including cardiovascular disease, and..."

Step 3: Elicit (Again)

Return the conversation to the patient immediately.

"What do you make of that?"

"How does that sit with you?"

"What questions does that raise for you?"

The second Elicit is the most commonly skipped step, and it is the most important one. Without it, E-P-E collapses into "E-P," which is just advice-giving with a polite opening. The second Elicit transforms information delivery into a collaborative exchange and often produces change talk.

6.2 Reflective Listening Under Pressure

In an ideal world, you would have unlimited time to craft the perfect reflection. In the real world, you have about five seconds. The following techniques help you deliver meaningful reflections quickly.

The One-Line Mirror

When you are short on time and the patient has just said something important, offer a one-sentence reflection that captures the core.

Patient: "I've been eating terribly, not sleeping, working overtime, and my back is killing me. I don't even know where to start."

One-line mirror: "You're overwhelmed, and everything feels like it's piling up at once."

The one-line mirror does not try to capture every detail. It captures the emotional center. In the example above, the patient listed four specific problems. The clinician reflected the underlying feeling (overwhelm) rather than attempting to address each problem individually. This single reflection communicates understanding more effectively than a detailed review of each complaint ever could.

Reflect Emotion Over Content

When time is short, reflecting the feeling is almost always more impactful than reflecting the facts.

Say This: "That sounds really discouraging."

Not That: "So you've been eating poorly and not sleeping and working a lot."

The content reflection is technically accurate but emotionally flat. It tells the patient you heard the words. The emotion reflection tells the patient you heard the person.

Avoiding the Question Trap

The most common error among clinicians learning MI is asking five or six questions in a row without a single reflection. This happens because questions feel productive. They feel like you are "doing something." Reflections, by contrast, can feel passive, as though you are just repeating what the patient said. But reflections are doing more than questions in most MI encounters. They build trust, demonstrate understanding, and create the conditions in which change talk can emerge.

A practical corrective: after every question you ask, pause and offer at least one reflection before asking the next question. If you catch yourself in a string of questions, stop and reflect the last thing the patient said. This simple discipline will transform your conversations.

6.3 The Importance and Confidence Rulers in Practice

The rulers are among the most versatile tools in the brief MI toolkit. They can be introduced in under thirty seconds, and the information they produce can guide the rest of the encounter.

Introducing the Rulers

Keep the setup brief and conversational.

"I'd like to ask you a question that might seem a little unusual. On a scale of 0 to 10, where 0 means not at all important and 10 means the most important thing in your life right now, how important is it to you to get your blood pressure under control?"

The Follow-Up That Makes It Work

The ruler number itself is only moderately useful. The follow-up question is where the magic happens.

Always ask: "Why did you say [number] and not something lower?"

This question invites the patient to articulate reasons for caring about change, which is pure change talk. If the patient says 5, asking "Why not a 2?" produces: "Well, because my mother had a stroke, and I know I'm at risk, and I want to be around for my kids." Those are three distinct pieces of change talk generated by a single question.

Never ask: "Why not higher?"

This question invites the patient to articulate reasons for not caring, which is sustain talk. If the patient says 5, asking "Why not a 7?" produces: "Because I feel fine, and I don't think the medication is doing anything, and I don't like taking pills." Those are three distinct pieces of sustain talk. The direction of your follow-up question determines the direction of the conversation.

Using the Gap Diagnostically

When the importance score is high but the confidence score is low, the patient is motivated but feels unable. The clinical response is to address barriers, build self-efficacy, and create a plan that feels achievable. "What would make you feel more confident?" is the key question.

When the confidence score is high but the importance score is low, the patient is capable but not motivated. The clinical response is to evoke values, explore goals, and deepen the patient's connection to why this change matters.

When both scores are low, the patient is in precontemplation. The appropriate response is to respect their position, plant a seed, and maintain the relationship for future conversations.

Documenting for Continuity

Recording the ruler scores in the patient's chart (e.g., "Importance: 6/10, Confidence: 4/10 for daily walking") creates a baseline that can be revisited at subsequent visits. "Last time, you said your confidence for walking was a 4. Where is it now?" This simple continuity check demonstrates that you remember, you care, and the conversation is ongoing.

6.4 Offering a Menu of Options

When a patient is ready for planning but unsure what to do, offering a menu of two to three options preserves their autonomy while channeling your clinical expertise.

"Based on what we've talked about, there are a few paths we could consider. Some patients in your situation have found it helpful to [option A]. Others have preferred [option B]. And some have started with [option C]. Which of those appeals to you, or is there something else you've been thinking about?"

The menu works because it avoids the single directive ("You should do X"), which triggers the righting reflex, while still providing structure and guidance. The closing phrase ("or is there something else you've been thinking about?") is important. It signals that the patient's own idea is just as valid as the clinician's suggestions.

Say This: "There are a couple of approaches we could consider. One would be to start with a short daily walk. Another would be to focus on the meals first. A third would be to try the medication we discussed. What feels most doable to you?"

Not That: "You need to start exercising and eating better. Here's a plan."

6.5 The Art of the Micro-Commitment

A micro-commitment is one small, specific, time-bound action that the patient chooses and believes they can complete. It is the output of the PLAN phase and the bridge between conversation and behavior.

Why Small Beats Ambitious

Ambitious plans feel motivating in the moment ("I'm going to go to the gym five days a week!") but collapse under the weight of real life. Micro-commitments succeed because they are genuinely achievable, and success breeds confidence. A patient who successfully walks for ten minutes on Monday is more likely to walk again on Wednesday than a patient who planned to walk for forty-five minutes and did not make it off the couch.

The Micro-Commitment Formula

A strong micro-commitment answers four questions:

What will I do? (A specific behavior, not a general category)

When will I do it? (A specific time or trigger)

Where will I do it? (A specific place, if applicable)

How much? (A specific quantity or duration)

Example: "I will walk around the block after dinner on Tuesday and Thursday evening." This is specific (walking around the block), time-bound (after dinner, Tuesday and Thursday), and achievable.

Helping the Patient Self-Select

The micro-commitment must come from the patient, not the clinician. Your job is to help the patient identify what they are willing to do, not to assign homework.

"Of everything we've talked about today, what feels like the most realistic first step for you?"

"What is one thing you'd be willing to try this week?"

"If you were going to do just one small thing differently, what would it be?"

When the patient names their own commitment, they are far more likely to follow through than when a clinician prescribes one, even if the clinician's plan is technically superior. Ownership matters more than optimization.

6.6 Case Study: Rafael and the Stalled Evoking Phase

Background

Rafael Estrada has been using the template for three weeks. His OPEN and FOCUS phases work well. But when he reaches the EVOKE phase, the conversation loses momentum. His patient today, Mrs. Angela Petrov, is a 52-year-old woman with elevated cholesterol who has been reluctant to start a statin.

Presentation

Rafael asks the importance ruler: "On a 0-to-10 scale, how important is it to you to bring your cholesterol down?" Mrs. Petrov says: "Maybe a 5." Rafael does not know where to go. In the past, he would have launched into a speech about cardiovascular risk. Today, he remembers the rule: ask why not lower.

Response

"A 5. So it's not nothing. Why a 5 and not a 2?"

Mrs. Petrov: "Well, my mother died of a heart attack at 68. I'm 52 now. I don't want to go the same way."

Rafael reflects the change talk: "Your mother's heart attack is still with you. You don't want that to be your story too."

Mrs. Petrov: "No. I don't. But I also don't want to be on medication for the rest of my life."

Rafael offers a double-sided reflection: "You're wary of being dependent on a pill, and at the same time, you're carrying the memory of what happened to your mother and wanting to take a different path."

Mrs. Petrov pauses: "I guess the question is whether there's something I could try first before the medication."

Rafael sees the opening: "There are a couple of things that have helped other patients lower their cholesterol without medication right away. Would you like to hear about them?"

Mrs. Petrov agrees. Rafael briefly describes dietary changes and exercise, then closes the loop: "Which of those feels like something you could actually do?"

Mrs. Petrov commits to replacing her evening chips with mixed nuts for the next two weeks. Confidence: 8.

Teaching Points

- "Why not lower?" unlocked the change talk that was hidden behind the neutral-sounding number.

- The mother's heart attack was the emotional engine. Rafael did not introduce this motivation. He evoked it.

- The double-sided reflection validated both sides of the ambivalence, which gave Mrs. Petrov permission to move toward the change side.

- The micro-commitment (nuts instead of chips) is small, specific, and genuinely achievable. A confidence score of 8 signals strong likelihood of follow-through.

6.7 Chapter Summary

The micro-skills that power the 10-Minute MI Template, E-P-E, reflective listening under pressure, the rulers, the menu of options, and the micro-commitment, are learnable, practicable, and improvable. Each one has common pitfalls: lecturing instead of using E-P-E, asking too many questions without reflecting, following up the ruler in the wrong direction, offering one directive instead of a menu, and accepting vague commitments instead of specific ones. The "Say This / Not That" comparisons in this chapter provide a concrete starting point for practice.

The next chapter addresses what happens when the template meets the unpredictable reality of clinical practice: patients in precontemplation, patients who get upset, language barriers, multiple competing targets, and the clock running out.

Chapter 7.0: When the Template Meets Reality

Dr. Mina Khoury was four minutes into a well-structured MI conversation about smoking cessation when her patient, a 39-year-old electrician named Chris Brennan, leaned back in his chair and said: "Look, doc, I know you mean well, but I've heard all this before. Can you just refill my inhaler and let me go?" In that moment, the template was no longer relevant. The patient was no longer engaged. The plan Dr. Khoury had been working toward evaporated. What happened next would depend entirely on whether she could recognize what was happening and respond in a way that preserved the relationship, even if it meant abandoning the behavior-change conversation entirely.

This chapter is about the moments when the template meets the messiness of real clinical life. No framework, no matter how well designed, can account for every variable. Patients arrive in unexpected stages of change. They get upset. They do not speak the clinician's language. They have seven problems and want to talk about all of them. They want you to just tell them what to do. And sometimes, you simply run out of time. Each of these situations calls for an adaptation that is consistent with MI spirit but does not follow the template step by step.

By the end of this chapter, you should be able to:

1. Adapt the template when the patient is in precontemplation.
2. Recognize and respond to discord without escalating.
3. Adjust MI techniques for patients with language barriers or low literacy.
4. Navigate encounters with multiple competing behavior targets.
5. Respond MI-consistently when a patient asks for direct advice.
6. Recover gracefully when time runs out before the plan is complete.

7.1 What If the Patient Is in Precontemplation?

Not every patient is ready to talk about change. Some are unaware that a problem exists. Others are aware but see no reason to change. Still others have been forced into the visit by a spouse, an employer, or a court order. These patients are in precontemplation, and pushing them toward a change plan will backfire reliably.

When you identify a patient in precontemplation, shift the goal. You are no longer aiming for a micro-commitment. You are aiming to plant a seed and preserve the relationship.

The practical moves are: build rapport through genuine engagement. Explore the patient's perspective without challenging it. Offer information only with permission and without attachment to the outcome. Avoid pushing for any commitment. Close with an open door.

"I'm glad we had a chance to talk about this. It sounds like this isn't something you're looking to change right now, and that's completely your call. If it ever becomes something you want to explore, I'm here. In the meantime, is there anything else I can help with today?"

This is the "raincheck" close. It communicates three things: I respect your autonomy. I am not giving up on you. The door is open whenever you are ready.

The temptation with precontemplative patients is to deliver one last piece of compelling information ("But did you know that...?") in the hope of tipping the balance. Resist this temptation. Information delivered to a precontemplative patient who did not request it is received as a lecture and strengthens the status quo. Respecting the patient's position today makes it more likely that they will return to the conversation tomorrow.

7.2 What If the Patient Gets Upset?

Discord, as discussed in Chapter 4, is a signal that the therapeutic relationship is strained. Common triggers include the clinician moving too fast, raising a topic the patient is not ready to discuss, or inadvertently communicating judgment.

When you sense discord, stop what you are doing and attend to the relationship.

Reflect the Emotion

"I can tell this is hitting a nerve. That's not my intention, and I want to understand what's going on for you."

"It sounds like I've stepped into something that doesn't feel right. Tell me more about what you're feeling."

Apologize Without Defensiveness

"I think I may have pushed too hard on this. I apologize. That's not the kind of conversation I want us to have."

This is not weakness. It is strength. An apology for a misstep communicates that you value the relationship more than you value being right.

Emphasize Autonomy

"What you do with your health is entirely your decision. I'm not here to pressure you. I'm here to help if and when you want help."

Shift Back to Engagement

"Let me take a step back. What matters most to you right now?"

In the scenario that opened this chapter, Dr. Khoury's patient said: "Can you just refill my inhaler and let me go?" An MI-consistent response might be: "Of course. I can do that right now. And I'm sorry if I came at the smoking conversation in a way that didn't feel right. I'll always respect where you are with it." This response fulfills the patient's request, acknowledges the misstep, and leaves the door open for future conversations. It turns a potentially relationship-damaging moment into a relationship-building one.

> **Teaching Point:** *Discord is not failure. It is feedback. Every experienced MI practitioner has triggered discord. What distinguishes a skilled practitioner from a novice is not that they avoid discord entirely, but that they recognize it immediately and repair it gracefully.*

7.3 What If There Is a Language Barrier or Low Literacy?

MI's reliance on verbal nuance creates challenges when the patient and clinician do not share fluent communication. The following adaptations can help.

Simplify Language

Replace clinical terms with everyday words. Instead of "How important is medication adherence to you?" try "How much does it matter to you to take your medicine every day?"

Adapt the Rulers

For patients who are not comfortable with numerical scales, use visual or gestural alternatives:

"Can you show me with your hands how much this matters to you? This far apart means it matters a lot. This far means not much."

"Point to the face that matches how you feel about making this change." (Use a simple faces scale from unhappy to happy.)

Work With Interpreters MI-Consistently

When using an interpreter, brief them before the encounter: "I'm going to be asking open-ended questions and reflecting what the patient says. Please translate as closely as possible, including the patient's exact words and tone, not just the content."

Speak in short sentences. Pause after each statement to allow for accurate translation. Maintain eye contact with the patient, not the interpreter. This communicates that the conversation is between you and the patient, with the interpreter as a bridge.

Use Visual Aids

Simple diagrams, emoji scales, or picture-based decision aids can replace or supplement verbal communication. A one-page visual showing the 10-minute template phases with icons can help orient a patient who has low literacy but good visual processing.

7.4 What If You Have Multiple Behavior Targets?

Mrs. Reyes in Chapter 5 had six overdue care plan items. In a single encounter, Dr. Okafor chose one. This is often the hardest decision in brief MI: which behavior to focus on when there are many competing priorities.

The agenda map technique resolves this by giving the patient the choice.

"I see a few things we could talk about today: your blood pressure medication, the exercise we discussed last time, the smoking, and whatever else is on your mind. Here they are." (You can write them on a whiteboard or list them verbally.) "Which one feels most important to you today?"

When the patient chooses, they are invested. The topics they did not choose are not abandoned. They are acknowledged and scheduled.

"Great, let's focus on the exercise today. And let's plan to come back to the medication conversation next time. Sound good?"

This approach respects the patient's autonomy, reduces overwhelm, and produces better outcomes on the chosen topic than a scattered conversation about all topics would produce on any of them.

7.5 What If the Patient Just Wants You to Tell Them What to Do?

Some patients arrive with a clear request: "Just tell me what I should eat." "What medication do you recommend?" "What should I do?" This is not resistance. It is trust. The patient is asking for your expertise. Dismissing the request with "Well, what do you think?" can feel evasive and undermine the relationship.

The MI-consistent response honors the request while still evoking the patient's own input.

"I appreciate you trusting me to weigh in. I'm happy to share what I've seen work for other patients. But first, can I ask: what have you already tried, and what's worked and what hasn't? That way, I can tailor my suggestions to what fits your life."

This response does three things. It affirms the patient (I appreciate your trust). It commits to sharing expertise (I'm happy to share). And it opens space for the patient's own experience (what have you tried?). From here, you can use E-P-E to deliver clinical recommendations within a collaborative frame.

After sharing recommendations, close with: "Of those options, what stands out as something that could work for you?" This returns the decision to the patient and ensures the plan is genuinely theirs.

7.6 What If You Lose Track of Time?

The clock is the enemy of good clinical conversations. Even with the best time management, you will sometimes reach the seven-minute mark of a ten-minute encounter and realize you are still in the EVOKE phase, with no plan in sight.

The Two-Minute Warning

When you notice time running short, signal the transition explicitly.

"We're getting close to the end of our time, and I want to make sure we wrap up in a useful way. Let me pull together what we've talked about."

Then deliver a transitional summary, emphasizing the change talk the patient has produced:

"Here's what I've heard today. You're concerned about your blood sugar, and you've noticed that when you eat more home-cooked meals, you feel better.

You're also juggling a lot with your mother's care and your own work schedule. Is there one small thing you'd be willing to try before I see you next?"

If the patient offers a commitment, check confidence and close. If the patient is not ready for a commitment, close with affirmation and an open door:

"I'm glad we started this conversation. It's clearly something you're thinking about. Let's keep talking about it next time."

Why Partial Is Better Than None

A common worry is that an incomplete template, one that reaches EVOKE but not PLAN, is a failure. It is not. Research on MI shows that the process of evoking change talk is itself therapeutic. A patient who spends seven minutes articulating their own reasons for change, even without a formal plan, has shifted their internal balance in the direction of change. That shift may produce action between visits, or it may set the stage for a productive planning conversation at the next encounter. In either case, the seven minutes were well spent.

7.7 Chapter Summary

The 10-Minute MI Template is a framework, not a cage. Real clinical encounters do not follow scripts, and the template must be adapted to the patient in front of you. When the patient is in precontemplation, shift from planning to seed-planting and use the raincheck close. When discord arises, reflect the emotion, apologize if needed, emphasize autonomy, and return to engagement. When language barriers or low literacy are present, simplify language, adapt rulers to visual formats, and work with interpreters thoughtfully. When multiple behavior targets compete, use the agenda map to let the patient choose. When the patient requests directive advice, honor the request using E-P-E. When time runs out, deliver a transitional summary and close with affirmation.

The unifying principle across all of these adaptations is MI spirit: compassion, acceptance, partnership, and evocation. When you are unsure what to do next, return to the spirit. Ask yourself: "Am I treating this person as a partner? Am I evoking rather than imposing? Am I respecting their autonomy?" If the answers are yes, you are on the right path, even if the template's clock has run out.

This concludes Part Two: The 10-Minute Framework. Part Three applies the framework to specific clinical settings and populations, beginning with primary care.

PART THREE: APPLIED SETTINGS AND POPULATIONS

Chapter 8.0: Brief MI in Primary Care

Dr. Samuel Osei had been in family medicine for eleven years. He knew the evidence for motivational interviewing. He had attended a workshop three years ago and remembered the general principles. But when he sat down with Mrs. Patricia Hawkins, a 63-year-old woman with type 2 diabetes who had gained eighteen pounds since her last visit and whose A1C had risen from 7.4 to 9.1, his first instinct was to pull up her lab results and explain, in careful detail, why these numbers were alarming. He caught himself. He had done exactly that at her last two visits, and nothing had changed. This time, he tried something different. He put the lab results aside, looked at Mrs. Hawkins, and said: "Before we get into the numbers, I'd like to hear from you. How have things been going?"

That question changed the entire visit. What followed was a ten-minute conversation that uncovered grief (her sister had died four months ago), isolation (she had stopped attending her church group), and a quiet admission that she had been eating for comfort because nothing else brought relief. None of this was in her chart. None of it would have surfaced if Dr. Osei had led with the lab values. And all of it was directly connected to the clinical outcomes he was trying to improve.

This chapter applies the 10-Minute MI Template to the five most common behavior-change targets in primary care: medication adherence, smoking cessation, alcohol and substance use screening, chronic disease self-management, and preventive screening conversations. Each section includes a clinical vignette that demonstrates the template in action. The goal is not to replace clinical judgment but to show how the template provides a reliable structure for conversations that clinicians have every day but rarely have a framework for conducting well.

By the end of this chapter, you should be able to:

1. Apply the 10-Minute MI Template to medication adherence conversations.
2. Integrate MI with the Five A's framework for smoking cessation.
3. Use MI-consistent language when introducing substance use screening results.
4. Adapt the template for chronic disease follow-up visits anchored by lab results.

5. Navigate preventive screening conversations with patients who are hesitant or fearful.

8.1 Medication Adherence

Medication non-adherence is one of the most pervasive and costly problems in healthcare. Approximately 50 percent of patients with chronic conditions do not take their medications as prescribed, and this figure has remained remarkably stable across decades of research and intervention efforts (Sabaté, 2003). The consequences are significant: uncontrolled chronic disease, avoidable hospitalizations, and an estimated $100 to $300 billion in excess healthcare costs annually in the United States alone (Viswanathan et al., 2012).

The reasons patients do not take their medications are diverse and often layered. Cost is a factor for many, particularly for patients on multiple chronic medications without adequate insurance coverage. Side effects, whether experienced or anticipated, deter others. Health beliefs play a role: some patients do not believe the medication is necessary, particularly for conditions that are asymptomatic, like hypertension and hyperlipidemia. Forgetfulness is common, especially among older adults managing complex regimens. Low health literacy means some patients do not fully understand what the medication does or how to take it correctly.

The traditional clinical response to non-adherence is education: explain the medication, explain the disease, explain the consequences of not taking it. This approach assumes that the problem is a knowledge deficit. In most cases, it is not. The patient usually knows the medication is important. The barriers are motivational, practical, or both. This is precisely the terrain where brief MI is most effective.

Clinical Vignette: Mr. Raymond Torres and the Statin

Mr. Torres is a 55-year-old construction foreman with hyperlipidemia. He was prescribed atorvastatin six months ago but stopped taking it after two weeks. His LDL is 188 mg/dL. He is here for a routine follow-up.

OPEN (Minutes 0 to 2):

"Good to see you, Mr. Torres. I know we have a few things to cover today, but I'd like to start with you. How have things been?"

Mr. Torres mentions work stress and a sore knee. He does not bring up the statin. Dr. Osei uses the permission question: "I noticed you haven't refilled the cholesterol medication in a while. Would it be all right if we talked about that for a few minutes?"

Mr. Torres shrugs: "Sure. I just stopped taking it. Didn't feel any different."

FOCUS (Minutes 2 to 4):

Dr. Osei reflects: "It's hard to stay motivated with a medication when you can't feel it working." He uses E-P-E: "What do you know about what the statin is supposed to do?" Mr. Torres says he knows it is for cholesterol. Dr. Osei provides briefly: "The tricky thing about cholesterol is that it does its damage silently, over years, by building up in the arteries. The statin slows that process down." He closes the loop: "What do you make of that?"

Mr. Torres: "I mean, I get it. But my dad had high cholesterol his whole life and he lived to 82."

EVOKE (Minutes 4 to 7):

Rather than arguing with the family history point, Dr. Osei asks: "On a 0-to-10 scale, how important is it to you to avoid a heart attack or stroke?" Mr. Torres says: "Maybe a 7." Dr. Osei follows up: "Why a 7 and not a 4?" Mr. Torres: "Because I've got two kids in high school. I need to be around." Dr. Osei reflects: "Your kids are your reason. You want to be there for them through the next chapter." Mr. Torres nods: "Yeah. I do."

PLAN (Minutes 7 to 10):

"You mentioned feeling like the medication wasn't doing anything. Would you be willing to try it again for 30 days and then recheck your cholesterol, so you can actually see the numbers change?" Mr. Torres agrees. Confidence check: "How confident are you that you can take it every day for 30 days?" He says 6. "What would bring it to a 7?" Mr. Torres: "If I took it at the same time every day. Maybe with my morning coffee." Dr. Osei affirms: "Coffee and a statin. You've already figured out the system. Let's see what the numbers look like in a month."

> **Teaching Point:** *The patient's father living to 82 with high cholesterol is sustain talk. Arguing against it ("But your father might have been lucky") would have produced more sustain talk. Dr. Osei sidestepped it by moving to the importance ruler, which shifted the conversation from the father's history to the patient's own values.*

8.2 Smoking Cessation

The Five A's framework (Ask, Advise, Assess, Assist, Arrange) has long been the standard approach for smoking cessation in primary care (Fiore et al., 2008). It is efficient, evidence-based, and widely taught. It also has a significant limitation: it works best with patients who are already motivated to quit. When a patient says "I'm not ready to quit," the Five A's framework offers little guidance beyond "Arrange for follow-up."

MI fills this gap. Specifically, MI provides tools for the "Assess" and "Assist" steps that go beyond readiness categorization and action planning. MI can help the clinician explore ambivalence, evoke the patient's own reasons for considering change, and create a micro-commitment that moves the conversation forward even when the patient is not ready for a quit date.

Clinical Vignette: Ms. Andrea Sloane and the "Not Ready" Smoker

Ms. Sloane is a 42-year-old office manager who smokes half a pack per day. She has smoked since age 19. At today's visit for a sinus infection, her chart flags a reminder to address tobacco use.

OPEN (Minutes 0 to 2):

After addressing the sinus infection, Dr. Chen says: "I see in your chart that you smoke. I bring this up with all my patients who smoke, not to lecture, but because I care about your health. Would it be all right to spend a couple of minutes on it?"

Ms. Sloane, visibly bracing: "I know I should quit. But I'm not ready."

FOCUS (Minutes 2 to 4):

Dr. Chen reflects: "You know it's something you should do, and right now isn't the time." She uses a double-sided reflection: "Smoking is giving you something, maybe stress relief, maybe a break during the day, and at the same time, there's a part of you that knows it's not serving your health."

Ms. Sloane: "It's the only thing that calms me down. I've tried quitting before and I was a nightmare."

EVOKE (Minutes 4 to 7):

Dr. Chen asks: "Tell me about that attempt. What worked, even for a little while?" Ms. Sloane describes cutting down to three cigarettes a day for two weeks using nicotine gum, then relapsing during a family crisis. Dr. Chen affirms: "You got down to three a day for two weeks. That took real effort." She follows with the importance ruler: "On a 0-to-10, how important is quitting to you at some point, not necessarily today, but eventually?" Ms. Sloane: "A 6." "Why not a 3?" "Because my mom had COPD. She was on oxygen for the last five years of her life. I don't want that."

PLAN (Minutes 7 to 10):

Dr. Chen does not push for a quit date. The patient is in contemplation, not preparation. Instead, she offers a menu: "Some patients in your situation have found it helpful to track their cigarettes for a week, just to notice patterns. Others have asked me to prescribe the nicotine gum so it's available when they're ready. And some just want to think about it and talk again at the next visit. Any of those appeal to you?"

Ms. Sloane chooses the gum prescription: "I'll have it on hand. Just in case."

Confidence check: "How confident are you that you'll fill the prescription?" "An 8. That part's easy. Using it is the hard part."

Dr. Chen closes: "You've been carrying your mom's story with you, and that says a lot about who you are and what you want for yourself. Whenever you're ready to use that gum, or to talk more about this, I'm here."

> **Teaching Point:** *The micro-commitment here is not quitting smoking. It is filling a prescription for nicotine gum. This is entirely appropriate for a patient in the contemplation stage. A commitment that matches the patient's readiness is always preferable to an ambitious commitment that will not be kept.*

8.3 Alcohol and Substance Use Screening

The SBIRT model (Screening, Brief Intervention, Referral to Treatment) provides a structured approach for identifying and addressing substance use in medical settings. Brief MI is a natural fit for the "Brief Intervention" component. However, the transition from screening to intervention is often the moment where conversations go wrong, because the way a clinician introduces a positive screening result can either open a dialogue or shut it down.

The most common error is leading with the score: "Your AUDIT score is 14, which means you're in the hazardous drinking range." This clinical framing often triggers shame, defensiveness, or disengagement. The patient may feel labeled, judged, or ambushed.

An MI-consistent approach introduces the results with curiosity rather than verdict.

"I'd like to share what came up on the questionnaire you filled out, and then I'd really like to hear your perspective. Would that be OK?"

After permission is granted, provide the result briefly: "The questionnaire suggests that your drinking pattern may be putting your health at some risk." Then immediately elicit: "What's your reaction to that?"

This sequence, permission, brief information, and open-ended elicitation, moves the conversation into MI territory before the patient has a chance to become defensive. From here, the standard template applies: explore ambivalence, evoke change talk, negotiate a micro-commitment if the patient is ready, or plant a seed if they are not.

Approaching the Topic Without Triggering Shame

The language you use matters enormously. Compare two approaches:

MI-Inconsistent: "Your screening shows you have a drinking problem. You need to cut back."

MI-Consistent: "The questionnaire flagged some things I'd like to understand better. I'm not here to judge. I just want to make sure we're looking at the full picture of your health. Can you tell me a bit about your relationship with alcohol?"

The second approach treats the patient as a person with a story, not a data point with a score. It invites narrative rather than defense. It creates the conditions for an honest conversation.

> **Teaching Point:** *SBIRT is a protocol. MI is a way of being. When you deliver SBIRT within the spirit of MI, the screening results become a conversation starter rather than a verdict. The patient is more likely to engage honestly, which makes the brief intervention more productive and the referral, if needed, more likely to be accepted.*

8.4 Chronic Disease Self-Management

Chronic disease management is, at its core, a behavior-change enterprise. Whether the condition is diabetes, hypertension, heart failure, or asthma, the clinical outcomes depend heavily on what the patient does between visits: taking medications, monitoring symptoms, adjusting diet, staying active, attending follow-up appointments. The clinician's role is to support the patient in doing these things consistently, which requires ongoing motivation, not just initial instruction.

The 10-Minute MI Template adapts well to the chronic disease follow-up visit, particularly when the visit is anchored by a lab result or a biometric measurement that can serve as a natural entry point for conversation.

Adapting the Template for a Lab-Result Visit

When you have a lab result to discuss, the temptation is to lead with the number. Resist that temptation and lead with the patient instead.

OPEN: "Before we look at the numbers, how have you been feeling about how things are going with your diabetes?"

This question gives the patient a chance to self-assess before being assessed. Their answer provides valuable context: a patient who says "I've been struggling" is in a different emotional place than one who says "I think I've been doing pretty well."

FOCUS: Introduce the lab result using E-P-E. "Your A1C came back at 8.4. Last time it was 7.8. What do you make of that?"

Notice that the clinician states the number but does not interpret it as good or bad. The patient's interpretation is more clinically useful than the clinician's judgment. A patient who says "That's not great, I've been slipping on my diet" has just produced change talk and identified the specific behavior that needs attention. A patient who says "I don't really know what that means" needs education before evoking.

EVOKE: "You mentioned that you've been slipping on the diet. On a 0-to-10 scale, how important is it to you to get that number back down?"

PLAN: "What's one thing you could realistically do this week to start moving in the right direction?"

The beauty of this approach in chronic disease management is its repeatability. Every follow-up visit becomes an opportunity to revisit the conversation, check progress, adjust the plan, and reinforce the patient's agency. Over time, these brief encounters build a cumulative narrative of collaboration and incremental change.

8.5 Preventive Screening Conversations

Preventive care conversations occupy a distinct space in the behavior-change landscape. The patient is not managing a diagnosed condition. They are being asked to do something, get a colonoscopy, receive a vaccine, complete an advance directive, that they may not see as urgent, relevant, or desirable. The motivational challenge is not adherence to a treatment. It is willingness to engage with a recommendation that may feel abstract, uncomfortable, or frightening.

MI helps in these conversations because it treats hesitancy as ambivalence rather than defiance. A patient who declines a flu vaccine is not necessarily "anti-vaccine." They may have concerns about side effects, a previous bad experience, mistrust of the healthcare system, or simply a feeling that the vaccine is not worth the inconvenience. MI explores these concerns rather than dismissing them.

Applying MI to Vaccination Hesitancy

Step 1: Ask permission. "I'd like to talk with you about the flu vaccine. Is that something you'd be open to discussing?"

Step 2: Elicit the patient's perspective. "What are your thoughts about getting the flu shot this year?"

Step 3: Listen and reflect. If the patient says "I got the flu shot once and it made me sick," reflect: "You had a bad experience, and that's stuck with you." Do not immediately correct the misconception. The patient will be more receptive to information after they feel heard.

Step 4: Provide information with permission. "Would it be helpful if I shared what we know about why that happens sometimes?" Then offer a brief, two-sentence explanation: "The flu shot can cause some aches and fatigue for a day or two, which is your immune system responding. It can't actually give you the flu, but I understand why it felt that way."

Step 5: Elicit response. "Knowing that, where does that leave you?"

This five-step sequence takes less than three minutes and applies to virtually any preventive screening conversation: cancer screening ("What have you heard about colonoscopy?"), advance directives ("Have you given any thought to what you'd want if you were too sick to make your own decisions?"), or health screening refusals of any kind.

> **Teaching Point:** *In preventive care, the clinician is often asking the patient to act on a risk that is statistical and future-oriented rather than immediate and personal. MI helps bridge this gap by connecting the recommendation to the*

> *patient's own values and concerns rather than relying on population-level statistics that feel impersonal.*

8.6 Pocket Summary: Primary Care Scenario Menu

Clinical Scenario	Template Entry Point	Key MI Move
Medication non-adherence	Permission question after chart review	Importance ruler: "Why that number and not lower?"
Smoking cessation (not ready)	Respectful agenda-setting; do not push for quit date	Menu of options; match commitment to stage
Positive substance use screen	E-P-E with screening result; elicit reaction	Curiosity over verdict; normalize ambivalence
Chronic disease follow-up with lab result	Lead with patient self-assessment before sharing numbers	E-P-E for lab results; one specific micro-commitment
Preventive screening hesitancy	Ask permission; elicit the patient's perspective first	Reflect concern before correcting misconception

8.7 Chapter Summary

Primary care is the setting where brief MI has the greatest potential for population-level impact, because it is where the most people are seen, the most chronic conditions are managed, and the most behavior-change conversations are either had or missed. The 10-Minute MI Template applies naturally to the five most common behavior-change targets in general medicine: medication adherence, smoking cessation, alcohol and substance use, chronic disease self-management, and preventive screening. In each case, the template provides a reliable structure that prevents the default to advice-giving and creates space for the patient's own motivation to emerge.

The consistent thread across all five scenarios is the same: lead with the patient, not the data. Whether the conversation begins with an LDL level, an AUDIT score, or a vaccination recommendation, the MI-consistent clinician puts the patient's perspective first and the clinical information second. This sequence is counterintuitive for many clinicians, but it is the single most reliable way to produce conversations that lead to actual behavior change.

The next chapter applies the template to the behavior changes most frequently addressed in health coaching and lifestyle medicine: diet, exercise, and weight management.

Chapter 9.0: Brief MI for Diet, Exercise, and Weight Management

Jasmine Tran was a certified health coach at a community wellness center. Her client, Mr. Dennis Kowalski, was a 49-year-old mail carrier whose physician had referred him for "diet and exercise counseling" after a borderline A1C of 6.3 and a blood pressure reading of 142/88. In their intake session, Jasmine had made a common mistake. She had asked Mr. Kowalski what he typically ate, listened politely, and then presented a sample meal plan with suggested substitutions. Mr. Kowalski had nodded through the entire thing, taken the handout, and never returned for a second session.

Three months later, when Mr. Kowalski was re-referred after his A1C rose to 6.5, Jasmine took a different approach. Instead of presenting a plan, she opened with: "What's been on your mind about your health since we last talked?" Mr. Kowalski's answer surprised her. He was not thinking about food at all. He was thinking about his father, who had been diagnosed with diabetes at 50 and had lost a toe to neuropathy at 62. "I keep wondering if I'm headed the same way," he said. Jasmine realized that the conversation about diet and exercise had to start not with a meal plan but with what mattered to Mr. Kowalski. The food would follow the motivation, not the other way around.

This chapter applies the 10-Minute MI Template to the behavior changes most frequently addressed in health coaching and lifestyle medicine: nutrition, physical activity, weight management, prediabetes, and the broader lifestyle factors of sleep and stress. The overarching principle is that lifestyle change conversations must be grounded in the patient's values, preferences, and readiness, not in the clinician's expertise about what they should be doing.

By the end of this chapter, you should be able to:

1. Conduct a nutrition conversation using MI-consistent language that avoids prescriptive lecturing.
2. Use OARS skills to explore barriers to physical activity and negotiate specific, achievable exercise commitments.
3. Navigate weight-related conversations with compassion and without shame.
4. Apply the importance ruler to lab values in prediabetes and metabolic syndrome conversations.

5. Expand lifestyle conversations beyond diet and exercise to include sleep and stress.

9.1 The MI Approach to Nutrition Conversations

"Eat more vegetables" is not behavior change counseling. It is advice, and it is the kind of advice that virtually every patient has already heard, often many times. The problem with generic dietary advice is not that it is wrong. It is that it is impersonal, unanchored, and disconnected from the patient's actual life. The patient who is told to eat more vegetables may be a single parent working two jobs with no time to cook, a truck driver who eats most meals at gas stations, or a person with a cultural food tradition that does not include the kind of salads their clinician has in mind. Telling them to eat more vegetables without understanding their context is like handing someone a map without knowing where they are starting from.

MI-consistent nutrition counseling begins not with what the patient should eat but with what they currently eat, what they enjoy, and what they would be willing to change.

The E-P-E Model for Nutrition

Step 1: Elicit the patient's current relationship with food.

"Tell me about how eating works in your life right now. What does a typical day look like?"

This open-ended invitation does something crucial: it centers the patient's experience. The answer reveals not just what they eat but why they eat it, what constraints shape their choices, and what foods bring them pleasure. All of this is essential data for constructing a plan that will actually be followed.

Step 2: Provide information briefly and with permission.

"Would it be helpful if I shared one thing that might make a noticeable difference, based on what you've described?"

The key word is "one." In a brief encounter, offering one targeted suggestion is more effective than a comprehensive dietary overhaul. The suggestion should be linked to something the patient said. If the patient mentioned eating fast food for lunch every day because the drive-through is on their route, a targeted suggestion might be: "Some patients in your situation have found that packing a sandwich the night before saves time and actually costs less than the drive-through."

Step 3: Elicit the patient's response.

"Does that seem like something that could work for you, or would something else fit your life better?"

This closing elicit is critical. It signals that the patient's judgment matters more than the clinician's recommendation. If the patient says "No, I can't do that because I don't have time in the evening," the clinician has learned something valuable and can adjust. If the patient says "Actually, I used to do that and it worked," the clinician has elicited change talk.

Common Trap: The Meal Plan Handout

Many clinicians and health coaches have access to standardized meal plans and feel compelled to distribute them. There is nothing inherently wrong with a meal plan, but handing it over without MI framing is the nutritional equivalent of the righting reflex. The patient receives a document full of foods they may not like, cannot afford, or do not know how to prepare, and the encounter feels like a transaction rather than a conversation. If you use a meal plan, integrate it with E-P-E: "I have a resource I can share, but first I'd like to understand what's realistic for your situation so we can figure out which parts, if any, would actually work for you."

9.2 Physical Activity and Exercise Initiation

Research consistently demonstrates that MI effectively supports physical activity initiation and maintenance by fostering intrinsic motivation and resolving ambivalence around common barriers (Frost et al., 2018). The barriers to exercise are among the most frequently cited in health behavior research: lack of time, physical pain or discomfort, embarrassment about appearance or fitness level, past failures that have eroded confidence, and the perception that exercise must be vigorous and sustained to "count."

MI addresses these barriers not by arguing against them (which activates the righting reflex) but by exploring them with curiosity and helping the patient find their own path through them.

Using OARS for Exercise Barriers

When a patient says "I don't have time to exercise," the MI-consistent response is not "Everyone can find 10 minutes" (which invalidates their experience). It is a reflection followed by an open question.

Reflection: "Your schedule is packed, and exercise feels like one more thing you don't have room for."

Open question: "If time weren't the issue, what kind of movement would you actually enjoy?"

This sequence accomplishes two things. The reflection validates the barrier, which reduces defensiveness. The open question shifts the frame from "exercise as obligation" to "movement as choice," and it often elicits surprising answers. The patient who says they have no time for exercise may reveal that they used to love dancing, or that they enjoy walking the dog, or that they would swim if there were a pool nearby. These are the seeds of a micro-commitment.

Specificity in Exercise Micro-Commitments

The difference between a commitment that is kept and one that is forgotten often comes down to specificity. Compare:

Vague: "I'll try to be more active."

Specific: "I'll walk to the mailbox and back after dinner on Monday, Wednesday, and Friday."

The specific commitment names the behavior (walking to the mailbox and back), the time (after dinner), and the days (Monday, Wednesday, Friday). It is small enough to be genuinely achievable and concrete enough to be remembered. The patient can evaluate at the end of the week whether they did it or not, which creates a foundation for the next conversation.

> **Teaching Point:** *Many patients carry a hidden belief that exercise only "counts" if it involves a gym, special clothing, or sustained effort. This belief can be a significant barrier to initiation. MI can help surface and challenge this belief gently. "It sounds like you have a picture of what exercise is supposed to look like, and it doesn't fit your life. What if we started with something that looks nothing like that picture?"*

9.3 Weight Management Without Shame

Weight is perhaps the most emotionally charged topic in lifestyle medicine. Many patients have internalized years of stigma, failed diets, and clinical encounters that made them feel judged. For these patients, a conversation about weight that begins with "You need to lose weight" is not just unhelpful. It is harmful. It reinforces shame, triggers defensive withdrawal, and damages the therapeutic relationship.

MI's compatibility with a weight-inclusive, health-at-every-size-informed approach is one of its greatest strengths in this domain. MI does not require the clinician to set a weight-loss target. It requires the clinician to explore what the patient wants, what matters to them, and what they are willing to do. If the patient identifies weight loss as a goal, MI supports that goal through the patient's own motivation. If the patient identifies improved energy, better sleep, or the ability to play with their grandchildren as goals, MI supports those goals directly, and the behaviors that serve those goals (dietary changes, increased movement) may or may not produce weight loss as a secondary outcome.

Focusing on Behaviors Rather Than the Scale

An MI-consistent approach to weight management shifts the conversation from outcomes (pounds lost) to behaviors (actions taken). This shift is both clinically sound and motivationally strategic.

MI-Inconsistent: "You've gained twelve pounds since your last visit. We need to talk about a weight loss plan."

MI-Consistent: "I want to check in on how things have been going for you in terms of eating, moving, and how you're feeling overall. What's been your experience?"

The second approach does not ignore the weight gain. It contextualizes it within the patient's broader experience. The patient may volunteer that they have been stress-eating since a job loss, that they have been unable to walk because of knee pain, or that they have been depressed and isolated. Each of these revelations opens a more productive conversation than "You need to lose weight" ever could.

Navigating the Sensitive Territory

When a patient has a strong emotional reaction to weight-related conversations, the MI practitioner's first job is to reflect the emotion, not to fix the problem.

Patient: "Every doctor I've ever seen has told me to lose weight. I'm so tired of hearing it."

Clinician: "You've heard this message over and over, and it's exhausting. It doesn't feel like anyone is really listening to what your life is actually like."

This reflection validates the patient's experience and opens the door to a different kind of conversation, one in which the patient feels seen as a person rather than a body mass index. From this foundation, the clinician can ask: "If we set the scale aside for a moment, what matters most to you about your health?" The patient's answer will be the foundation for an MI-consistent plan that the patient actually owns.

9.4 Prediabetes and Metabolic Syndrome

The Diabetes Prevention Program (DPP) trial demonstrated that lifestyle intervention, primarily modest weight loss through dietary change and physical activity, reduces the risk of progression from prediabetes to type 2 diabetes by 58 percent, a result that exceeded the effect of metformin (Knowler et al., 2002). This finding has made prediabetes one of the most important targets for brief behavioral intervention in primary care and health coaching.

MI plays a natural role in prediabetes management because the conversation involves persuading an otherwise-well person to change behaviors in response to a risk that is statistical and future-oriented. The patient does not feel sick. They may not understand what "prediabetes" means. They may have heard the term and assumed it is either trivial ("pre" sounds like "not yet") or terrifying ("diabetes runs in my family and now it's happening to me"). Either interpretation creates motivational challenges that generic advice cannot address.

Using the Importance Ruler with Lab Values

The importance ruler becomes especially powerful when paired with a specific clinical number.

"Your A1C came back at 6.2, which puts you in the prediabetes range. On a scale of 0 to 10, how important is it to you to bring that number down?"

The patient may say "8" (high importance, proceed to planning) or "3" (low importance, explore values and goals before proceeding). Either answer gives the clinician critical information about where to focus the remaining minutes of the conversation.

If the patient says a high number, follow with: "What would you be willing to try in the next two weeks to start moving that number?"

If the patient says a low number, follow with: "What would need to change for that number to feel more important to you?" This question often reveals underlying beliefs ("I don't think diet makes that much difference") or competing priorities ("I'm dealing with my mother's hospice care right now") that must be acknowledged before any behavior-change conversation can be productive.

9.5 Sleep, Stress, and Whole-Person Lifestyle

Diet and exercise dominate lifestyle medicine conversations, but they are often not the primary drivers of a patient's health behavior struggles. Sleep deprivation, chronic stress, and emotional exhaustion frequently undermine efforts to eat well and stay active. A patient who sleeps five hours per night is neurobiologically predisposed to crave high-calorie foods, lack the energy for exercise, and make impulsive decisions about their health (Walker, 2017). A patient who is chronically stressed may use food, alcohol, or sedentary behavior as coping mechanisms, and no amount of nutritional education will change those patterns until the stress itself is addressed.

Brief MI for sleep and stress follows the same template as brief MI for any other behavior, but the OPEN phase may need to be more exploratory.

"When we think about lifestyle changes, people usually jump to food and exercise. But I'm curious about the bigger picture. How are you sleeping? How are you managing stress?"

This question signals to the patient that you see them as a whole person, not just a set of lab values. It also opens the door to conversations that may reveal the root causes of the dietary and exercise patterns that appear in the chart.

Brief MI for Sleep Hygiene

Sleep conversations lend themselves well to MI because most patients already know what they "should" be doing (going to bed at a consistent time, avoiding screens before bed, limiting caffeine) but are not doing it. The gap between knowledge and behavior is a motivational gap, not an information gap.

"You mentioned you're only sleeping about five hours a night. On a 0-to-10 scale, how important is it to you to improve that?"

If importance is high, move to a micro-commitment: "What's one small thing you could try this week to get even 30 more minutes of sleep?"

If importance is low, explore: "What gets in the way of making sleep a priority?" The answer often reveals competing demands (caregiving, work schedule, a partner who snores) that contextualize the problem and open new avenues for problem-solving.

Brief MI for Stress Management

Stress conversations require particular sensitivity because stress is often intertwined with life circumstances the patient cannot easily change (poverty, caregiving responsibilities, unsafe housing, workplace demands). MI respects this reality by not suggesting that the patient "just manage their stress better" but instead exploring what is within their control.

"It sounds like you're carrying a lot right now. Of all the things on your plate, what is one small piece that you could take some pressure off?"

This question honors the complexity of the patient's situation while still moving toward agency and action.

9.6 Case Study: Jasmine and Mr. Kowalski Revisited

Background

Jasmine Tran, the health coach from the opening vignette, has Mr. Kowalski back in her office after his A1C rose to 6.5. He is a 49-year-old mail carrier referred for diet and exercise counseling.

Presentation

Mr. Kowalski is cooperative but skeptical. His first session ended with a meal plan he never used. He is carrying the weight of his father's diabetes history.

Analysis

Mr. Kowalski's readiness is in early contemplation. He is aware of the risk but has not connected it to specific behavioral intentions. His previous experience (meal plan handed to him without exploration of his context) reinforced a sense that health professionals do not understand his life. His father's story is a powerful motivational resource that was never accessed in the first session.

Response

Jasmine opens with: "Last time we met, I gave you a meal plan without really understanding your situation. I want to do this differently today. Can you tell me about what matters most to you when you think about your health?"

Mr. Kowalski talks about his father. Jasmine reflects: "Watching your father go through that, losing part of his foot, being limited, that's not something you want for yourself." Mr. Kowalski: "No. Absolutely not." Jasmine follows with the importance ruler: "On a 0-to-10, how important is it to you to avoid going down that same road?" He says 9.

Jasmine asks: "You said 9. That's very high. What would help you start making changes that match how strongly you feel about this?" Mr. Kowalski identifies two things: he wants to stop drinking soda during his mail route (he drinks three cans a day), and he wants to walk on his days off instead of watching television.

Confidence check for soda: "How confident are you that you could switch to water during your route?" He says 5. "What would bring it to a 7?" He suggests bringing a water bottle from home and keeping it in his truck. Confidence rises to 7.

Confidence check for walking: 8. No adjustment needed.

Outcome

At his two-week follow-up, Mr. Kowalski had eliminated soda on work days (switching to water) and walked three times on his days off. His wife joined him for two of the walks. He reported feeling "more in control." His A1C at the three-month check: 6.1.

Teaching Points

- The meal plan approach failed because it bypassed the patient's context and motivation. The MI approach succeeded because it started with what mattered to the patient.

- The father's diabetes history was the emotional fuel for change. It was present at the first visit but never accessed because Jasmine led with the plan instead of the person.

- Two specific, achievable micro-commitments (water instead of soda, walking on days off) produced measurable clinical improvement in three months.

- Confidence troubleshooting (bringing a water bottle) turned a shaky 5 into a workable 7.

9.7 Pocket Summary: MI Questions Mapped to the Template

Template Phase	Diet Questions	Exercise Questions	Sleep Questions	Stress Questions
OPEN	"Tell me about how eating works in your life."	"What role does movement play in your daily routine?"	"How have you been sleeping?"	"What's been weighing on you lately?"
FOCUS	"If you could change one thing about your eating, what would it be?"	"What kind of movement have you enjoyed in the past?"	"What gets in the way of better sleep?"	"Of everything on your plate, what is one piece you could address?"
EVOKE	"On 0-to-10, how important is changing your eating habits?"	"What would be different if you were more active?"	"On 0-to-10, how important is improving your sleep?"	"What would your life look like with less of this pressure?"
PLAN	"What's one small change you'd be willing to try this week?"	"What specific movement could you commit to before our next visit?"	"What's one thing you could try tonight to sleep better?"	"What is one small thing you could do this week to take care of yourself?"

9.8 Chapter Summary

Diet, exercise, and weight management are the most frequently addressed behavior-change targets in health coaching and lifestyle medicine, and they are among the most resistant to change through advice-giving alone. MI provides a framework for these conversations that respects the patient's autonomy, explores their context, and elicits their own motivation before offering any recommendations. The E-P-E model prevents nutritional lecturing. The OARS skills surface exercise barriers and generate specific, achievable commitments. A compassionate, behavior-focused approach to weight avoids shame and preserves the therapeutic relationship. The importance ruler connects lab values to personal motivation in prediabetes conversations. And expanding the conversation to include sleep and stress often reveals the root causes that diet and exercise interventions alone cannot address.

The next chapter adapts the 10-Minute MI Template for the health coaching and wellness program context, including corporate wellness, telehealth, and community health worker encounters.

Chapter 10.0: Brief MI in Health Coaching and Wellness Programs

Elena Vargas was six months into her role as a health coach for a large technology company's employee wellness program. Her caseload included 45 employees, most of whom had been "voluntold" by their managers to participate after the company's health risk assessment revealed elevated rates of obesity, hypertension, and sedentary behavior. Elena's first challenge was not teaching people to eat better or move more. Her first challenge was that half of her clients did not want to be there.

Marcus, a 36-year-old software engineer, arrived at his initial coaching session with his arms crossed and his phone face-up on the table. "My manager said I had to do this," he said. "So here I am." Elena had two options. She could launch into the wellness program's goals, explain the health benefits of participation, and outline the coaching schedule. Or she could start with Marcus. She chose Marcus.

"I appreciate you showing up, even if it wasn't your idea. I'm curious: setting aside what your manager wants, is there anything about your health that you've been thinking about on your own?"

Marcus's posture softened slightly. "I've been getting headaches. And I'm tired all the time, but I sleep eight hours." That opening, small as it was, became the foundation for a coaching relationship that eventually addressed sleep quality, caffeine consumption, screen breaks, and physical activity, all on Marcus's terms, in his own time.

This chapter adapts the 10-Minute MI Template for the health coaching context, including corporate wellness programs, telehealth and digital coaching, and community health worker encounters. Health coaches have a significant advantage over many clinical settings: more time per session, ongoing relationships, and a broader mandate that includes whole-person wellness. The template is not meant to replace a full coaching session. It is meant to function as a micro-cycle within it, a structured segment that can be used once or multiple times within a longer engagement.

By the end of this chapter, you should be able to:

1. Distinguish between motivational interviewing and health coaching and describe how they complement each other.

2. Structure a 30-minute coaching session using two to three template micro-cycles.
3. Adapt MI techniques for reluctant participants in corporate wellness programs.
4. Modify the template for telehealth and phone-based coaching encounters.
5. Train non-licensed community health workers in the brief MI template.

10.1 MI and Health Coaching: Overlapping but Distinct

Motivational interviewing and health coaching share a philosophical foundation: both are person-centered, both respect autonomy, and both aim to support sustainable behavior change. They are often described as though they are the same thing, but they are not. Understanding the distinction clarifies how they work together.

MI is a communication style designed to be brief and focused. Its primary purpose is to strengthen a person's own motivation and commitment to change. MI is typically used in one to three sessions and is intended to address a specific behavior. Once the person has developed sufficient motivation and a concrete plan, MI's work is largely done, and other approaches may take over (Simmons & Wolever, 2013).

Health coaching, by contrast, is a comprehensive intervention. It unfolds over multiple sessions (typically six or more), addresses the whole person, helps clients develop a vision for their health, identifies core values, and supports the client through the entire change process, from contemplation through sustained maintenance. Health coaching does not end when the plan is made. It continues through implementation, troubleshooting, and long-term habit formation.

The synergy between MI and coaching is that MI provides the communication spine of a coaching practice. MI's skills (OARS, change talk elicitation, the importance ruler, E-P-E) are the tools a coach uses to navigate the most critical moments in any session: the moments when the client is ambivalent, stuck, or uncertain. The 10-Minute MI Template can function as a micro-cycle within a longer coaching session, used whenever the conversation arrives at a point of motivational decision.

10.2 Structuring a Coaching Session with the Template

A typical health coaching session lasts 30 to 45 minutes. Within that time, a coach might use the 10-Minute MI Template two or three times, each cycle addressing a different aspect of the client's situation.

Sample Structure for a 30-Minute Session:

Minutes 0 to 5: Check-In and Agenda-Setting

"How have things been since we last talked? What would you like to focus on today?"

Minutes 5 to 15: First MI Micro-Cycle

Apply the full template (OPEN, FOCUS, EVOKE, PLAN) to the client's primary concern. If the client wants to discuss exercise, spend ten minutes using MI to explore barriers, evoke motivation, and negotiate a specific commitment.

Minutes 15 to 25: Second MI Micro-Cycle

Address a secondary topic or deepen the first one. If the exercise conversation revealed that stress is the underlying barrier, spend the second cycle on stress management using MI.

Minutes 25 to 30: Summary and Forward Planning

Collect the session's key themes, summarize commitments, and set the agenda for the next session.

This structure allows the coach to maintain the relational, person-centered quality of a coaching session while using MI's focused, strategic techniques at the points where they are most needed. The template provides direction without rigidity. It ensures that each micro-cycle has a clear purpose (evoking, planning) rather than drifting into unfocused conversation.

> **Teaching Point:** *Not every moment in a coaching session requires MI. There are times when the coach is primarily listening, educating, or problem-solving. The template is for the moments of motivational decision: when the client is weighing change, expressing ambivalence, or negotiating a commitment. Recognizing when to deploy the template and when to set it aside is an important coaching skill.*

10.3 Corporate Wellness and Employee Health

Corporate wellness programs create a unique motivational context because participation is often externally driven rather than internally motivated. Employees may be participating because their employer requires it, because they receive a premium discount for completing a health assessment, or because their manager "strongly encouraged" them to attend. None of these motivations are intrinsic, and the MI practitioner must navigate the resulting ambivalence with particular care.

Working with the Reluctant Participant

The most important move with a reluctant participant is to acknowledge the situation honestly and without judgment.

"I know this wasn't your idea. A lot of people in your position feel the same way. I'm not going to try to convince you to do something you don't want to do. But I am curious: is there anything about your own health that you've been thinking about, separate from what brought you here?"

This statement does several things. It normalizes the reluctance. It explicitly removes the pressure to comply. And it opens a door to intrinsic motivation by distinguishing between the employer's agenda and the employee's own concerns. If the employee identifies something, even something small ("I've been getting winded going up stairs"), you have a collaborative starting point. If they identify nothing ("No, I'm good"), respect that answer, use the session to build rapport, and leave the door open for future conversations.

When the Employer's Goals and the Employee's Goals Do Not Align

A company may want its employees to lose weight and exercise more. An employee may want to manage anxiety, improve sleep, or deal with a difficult manager. These goals are not necessarily in conflict, anxiety management and sleep improvement both contribute to physical health, but they require the coach to honor the employee's stated priorities rather than imposing the company's.

"The wellness program has some specific goals around physical activity and nutrition. But the most effective coaching I've done starts with what matters most to you. If we address what's really on your mind, the other pieces often fall into place. What would you like to focus on?"

10.4 Telehealth and Digital Coaching

The rapid expansion of telehealth and digital coaching has created new opportunities for MI delivery and new challenges for MI practitioners. The fundamental skills of MI, OARS, change talk elicitation, reflective listening, work on any platform. But the medium introduces complications that require conscious adaptation.

Challenges of Virtual MI

Limited nonverbal cues. On a phone call, the coach cannot see facial expressions, posture shifts, or eye contact. On a video call, these cues are present but diminished by screen size, camera angle, and bandwidth. Subtle emotional responses that would be obvious in person may be missed.

Connectivity disruptions. A dropped connection during a critical reflection or a moment of emotional disclosure can derail the conversation's momentum.

Screen fatigue. Clients who spend their workday on video calls may arrive at a coaching session already depleted.

Distractions. Clients on phone calls may be driving, cooking, or multitasking.

Adaptations for Virtual MI

More frequent summaries. In the absence of full nonverbal feedback, the coach must check understanding more often. "Let me make sure I'm tracking with you. You said..." This serves the same function as a head nod in person: it signals attention and invites correction.

Deliberate pausing. Silence is one of MI's most powerful tools, but silence on a phone call can feel like a dropped connection. When you pause deliberately, name it: "I want to sit with what you just said for a moment." This prevents the client from thinking the line went dead.

Using the chat function for rulers. On video platforms, the importance and confidence rulers can be delivered via the chat function: "Type a number from 0 to 10: how important is this change to you?" This adds a visual element that anchors the conversation and gives the client a different mode of engagement.

Setting the container. Open every virtual session by establishing ground rules: "Can you find a quiet spot where we won't be interrupted for the next 30 minutes?" This simple request communicates that the session matters and helps the client transition from their digital workday into a reflective space.

10.5 Community Health Workers and Peer Specialists

Community health workers (CHWs) and peer specialists occupy a unique position in the healthcare ecosystem. They are trusted members of the communities they serve, often sharing language, culture, and lived experience with their clients. They are also, in most cases, non-licensed practitioners without formal training in psychotherapy or counseling. This combination of high trust and limited training makes brief MI an especially good fit for their work.

The evidence supports this. Studies have demonstrated that lay health workers can deliver brief MI with measurable positive effects on health behaviors, provided they receive adequate initial training and ongoing support (Martins & McNeil, 2009). The key is fidelity: ensuring that CHWs learn and maintain the core MI skills (OARS, E-P-E, the template structure) without drifting into advice-giving, which is the most common point of failure.

Training CHWs in the Brief MI Template

A practical approach to CHW training includes three phases:

Phase 1: Foundation (one to two days). Teach the MI spirit (CAPE), the four OARS skills, and the 10-Minute MI Template using lecture, demonstration, and role-play. Emphasize the spirit above all else: if the CHW does nothing but listen well and respect autonomy, they are already practicing MI-consistently.

Phase 2: Practice with feedback (two to four weeks). CHWs practice the template in real encounters and record (with permission) at least two sessions for review. A trainer or supervisor listens to the recordings and provides specific, constructive feedback on OARS skill use and template fidelity.

Phase 3: Ongoing support (monthly). Monthly group peer practice sessions of 30 to 60 minutes in which CHWs share challenges, practice skills in role-play, and receive encouragement. Without this ongoing support, skill drift is virtually guaranteed.

> **Teaching Point:** *The greatest asset CHWs bring to MI is trust. A patient who would not open up to a physician may disclose openly to a CHW who shares their cultural background and lived experience. MI gives CHWs a structure for turning that trust into productive behavior-change conversations. The structure protects against the most common CHW pitfall, which is well-intentioned but directive advice-giving that undermines the patient's autonomy.*

10.6 Case Study: Elena, Marcus, and the Reluctant Engineer

Background

Elena Vargas is a health coach in a corporate wellness program. Marcus, a 36-year-old software engineer, was required to attend by his manager. He arrives skeptical and disengaged.

Presentation

Marcus's body language is closed. He states that he is there because his manager told him to be. He does not identify any health concerns initially.

Analysis

Marcus is in precontemplation for most wellness program goals but reveals mild contemplation when Elena creates space for his own agenda: headaches and fatigue despite adequate sleep.

Response

Elena avoids the wellness program's scripted intake. Instead, she opens with curiosity: "Setting aside what your manager wants, is there anything about your health that you've been thinking about?" Marcus mentions headaches and fatigue. Elena reflects: "You're putting in the hours of sleep but not getting the recovery you'd expect." She asks: "What do you think is going on?"

Marcus identifies excessive caffeine (six cups of coffee by 2 PM), minimal water, and no breaks during his 10-hour coding sessions. Elena uses the importance ruler: "How important is it to you to figure out the headache and fatigue problem?" Marcus says 8.

Elena offers a menu: "Some people in your situation have found it helpful to cut caffeine after noon. Others start with adding a 10-minute walk between coding blocks. Others focus on hydration first. What appeals to you?"

Marcus chooses hydration: "I can keep a water bottle at my desk." Confidence: 9.

Elena closes: "You came in here because someone told you to. But you found something that actually matters to you, and you already have a plan. That's a strong start."

Outcome

Over four sessions, Marcus reduced caffeine to two cups daily, began taking afternoon walks, and reported significant improvement in headaches and energy. He never engaged with the wellness program's formal weight-loss goals, but his health risk assessment scores improved at the six-month mark.

Teaching Points

- Honoring the client's agenda (headaches and fatigue) rather than the employer's agenda (weight loss) produced engagement and measurable health improvement.

- The reluctant participant became willing when the conversation shifted from external obligation to internal concern.

- A confidence score of 9 for the hydration commitment predicted strong follow-through. Starting with a near-certain success builds momentum for harder changes later.

- MI does not require the client to pursue the "right" goals. It requires the clinician to follow the client's motivation wherever it leads.

10.7 Pocket Summary: Health Coaching Session Planner

Session Segment	Time	MI Function	Key Tools
Check-in and agenda-setting	0 to 5 min	Engaging, beginning of Focusing	Open-ended question, rapport building
MI Micro-Cycle 1: Primary concern	5 to 15 min	Full template (OPEN, FOCUS, EVOKE, PLAN)	Rulers, evocative questions, micro-commitment
MI Micro-Cycle 2: Secondary topic or deepening	15 to 25 min	Full or partial template	Double-sided reflection, E-P-E, troubleshooting
Summary and forward planning	25 to 30 min	Closing, transitional summary	Collecting summary, affirmation, next-session agenda

10.8 Chapter Summary

Health coaching and MI are distinct but deeply synergistic. MI provides the communication skills and motivational strategies that coaches deploy at the critical decision points within longer coaching engagements. The 10-Minute MI

Template functions as a micro-cycle within a 30-to-45-minute coaching session, providing structure and direction without replacing the broader coaching relationship. Corporate wellness settings require particular sensitivity to reluctant participants, and the MI practitioner must honor the employee's intrinsic concerns over the employer's programmatic goals. Telehealth coaching demands adaptations for limited nonverbal cues, including more frequent summaries, deliberate pausing, and creative use of chat functions. Community health workers, with their unique combination of community trust and non-specialist training, are strong candidates for brief MI delivery, provided they receive adequate initial training and ongoing support.

The next chapter extends the template to settings beyond primary care and health coaching: emergency departments, dental offices, pharmacies, pediatric clinics, and integrated behavioral health teams.

Chapter 11.0: Brief MI Across the Care Continuum

It was 2:17 AM when Dr. Priya Sharma walked into Bay 4 of the emergency department. The patient, a 28-year-old man named Tyler Briggs, had arrived by ambulance after collapsing at a bar. His blood alcohol level was 0.31. He had lacerations on his forehead from the fall. He was awake, oriented, and already asking when he could leave.

The standard ED approach to this encounter would be to stabilize the patient, suture the lacerations, observe until the alcohol level dropped, and discharge with a printed handout about alcohol misuse. Dr. Sharma had done this hundreds of times. The handout went into the trash roughly 100 percent of the time.

Tonight, she tried something different. After the sutures were done and Tyler was waiting for discharge, she sat down and said: "I've got a few minutes while we wait for your paperwork. Can I ask you something? What was tonight supposed to look like before things went sideways?"

Tyler paused. "I was celebrating. Got a promotion." Then, quieter: "My girlfriend was supposed to meet me there. She texted that she's done. That I always do this."

In ninety seconds, Dr. Sharma had learned more about Tyler's relationship with alcohol than a screening questionnaire could have revealed in ten minutes. The conversation that followed lasted five minutes and did not include a lecture, a pamphlet, or a referral. It included one reflection ("Tonight was supposed to be a celebration, and instead it cost you something important"), one evocative question ("What do you think your girlfriend means when she says you 'always do this'?"), and one seed planted ("If you ever want to talk to someone about the drinking, here's a number you can call. No pressure."). Tyler took the card.

This chapter extends the 10-Minute MI Template to five clinical settings beyond primary care and health coaching: emergency departments, dental practices, pharmacies, pediatric and adolescent health, and integrated behavioral health. In each setting, the time constraints are different, the patient populations have unique characteristics, and the template requires specific adaptations. What remains constant is the spirit of MI: compassion, acceptance, partnership, and evocation.

By the end of this chapter, you should be able to:

1. Use brief MI techniques during "reachable moments" in emergency and urgent care settings.
2. Apply MI to oral health behavior conversations in dental practice.
3. Deliver MI-consistent medication counseling at the pharmacy dispensing counter.
4. Adapt MI for pediatric and adolescent encounters, including working with parents.
5. Use MI language in warm handoffs and brief behavioral health consultations within integrated care teams.

11.1 Emergency Department and Urgent Care

The emergency department is an unlikely setting for behavior-change conversations, and that is precisely what makes it powerful. Patients arrive in the ED after acute events, overdoses, injuries, chest pain scares, alcohol-related falls, that temporarily strip away the denial, minimization, and routine that normally insulate them from confronting their behavior. This creates what researchers call a "reachable moment," a window of heightened openness to change that may not be present during a routine office visit (Bernstein et al., 2005).

The challenge is that the window is narrow. ED visits are chaotic. The patient may be in pain, intoxicated, frightened, or all three. The clinician may have five other patients waiting. There is no time for a full MI session. There is, however, time for a seed.

The Ultra-Brief Seed-Planting Encounter (2 to 5 Minutes)

Step 1: Name the moment. "Something brought you here tonight. I'd like to understand what happened."

Step 2: Reflect what matters. Listen for the thing the patient cares about most (their relationship, their job, their children, their freedom) and reflect it back.

Step 3: Plant the seed. One evocative question or one piece of information delivered with E-P-E.

Step 4: Leave the door open. "If you ever want to talk about this more, here's how you can reach someone." Provide a resource card or phone number without pressure.

This four-step sequence does not require the full template. It does not require a micro-commitment. It does not require the patient to be sober, calm, or cooperative. It requires only that the clinician seize a brief window of opportunity and use it to plant something that may grow later.

SBIRT in the ED

The SBIRT model has strong evidence in emergency settings, particularly for alcohol use. Studies have shown that even a single brief intervention in the ED can reduce alcohol consumption at follow-up (Academic ED SBIRT Research Collaborative, 2007). MI provides the communication framework for the "Brief Intervention" component, ensuring that the conversation is collaborative rather than confrontational and that the patient's autonomy is preserved even in a high-acuity, time-pressured environment.

11.2 Dental and Oral Health

Dental settings present a distinctive opportunity for brief MI because patients return regularly, the behaviors targeted (oral hygiene, sugar consumption, tobacco use) are directly observable, and the clinical encounter includes dedicated time for patient interaction during hygiene appointments.

Research supports the use of brief MI in dental practice. Studies have found that MI-based interventions improve oral hygiene behaviors, reduce sugar consumption, and support smoking cessation in dental patients, with effects maintained at follow-up (Cascaes et al., 2014; Yevlahova & Satur, 2009). The interventions studied were typically brief, lasting five to fifteen minutes, and were delivered by dental hygienists and dentists rather than specialized counselors.

Applying the Template in the Dental Chair

The dental hygiene appointment provides a natural structure for brief MI. The hygienist has five to ten minutes of conversation time during the cleaning, and the topics are clearly defined: brushing and flossing habits, dietary sugar, tobacco use, and appointment adherence.

OPEN: "How have things been going with your home care routine since your last visit?"

FOCUS: If the patient mentions difficulty flossing, focus there. "What gets in the way of flossing regularly?"

EVOKE: "On a 0-to-10 scale, how important is it to you to keep your teeth healthy as you age?" Follow-up: "Why that number and not lower?"

PLAN: "What's one small change you'd be willing to try before I see you next?" A micro-commitment for flossing might be: "I'll floss just my front teeth every night before bed." This is small, specific, and more achievable than "floss every tooth every day," which is the standard recommendation that most patients have already failed to follow.

> **Teaching Point:** *The dental setting benefits from MI's non-judgmental spirit because many patients feel shame about their oral health. A patient who has not flossed in months and sees bleeding gums in the mirror is already self-critical. Lecturing them about flossing compounds the shame. Reflecting their concern and affirming their presence at the appointment creates the conditions for honest conversation and realistic planning.*

11.3 Pharmacy and Medication Counseling

Pharmacists interact with more patients more frequently than almost any other healthcare provider, and most of those interactions include a medication-related behavior-change opportunity: a new prescription that requires adherence, a refill that reveals a gap in use, a question about side effects that signals ambivalence, or a patient picking up a medication for a newly diagnosed condition who is visibly overwhelmed.

The pharmacy counter is an extremely constrained environment. Conversations are brief (often two to three minutes), semi-public, and frequently interrupted. Yet even within these constraints, MI-consistent communication can make a meaningful difference.

The Pharmacist as Brief MI Practitioner

A pharmacist dispensing a new statin to a patient who seems uncertain might use the following two-minute MI sequence:

"I see this is a new medication for you. What has your doctor told you about it so far?" (Elicit)

Patient: "Something about cholesterol. I'm not sure I need it."

Pharmacist reflects: "You're not fully convinced this is necessary." (Reflection)

Patient: "I mean, I feel fine."

Pharmacist: "A lot of people feel that way, and it makes sense. The tricky part with cholesterol is that it doesn't cause symptoms until it's done damage. Would it be helpful if I explained what the medication does in about 30 seconds?" (E-P-E: permission)

Patient: "Sure."

Pharmacist provides a brief explanation, then closes: "Knowing that, where are you leaning in terms of giving it a try?" (Elicit)

This sequence takes less than two minutes and covers the essential MI moves: eliciting the patient's starting point, reflecting their concern, providing information with permission, and returning the decision to the patient. It is not a comprehensive MI session. It is a seed, planted in fertile soil, that may germinate over the coming days as the patient decides whether to open the bottle.

Medication Therapy Management (MTM)

In the context of MTM encounters, pharmacists have more time (typically 15 to 30 minutes) and a more structured setting. The full 10-Minute MI Template can be applied directly to MTM conversations about adherence, polypharmacy management, and lifestyle modifications that complement pharmacotherapy.

11.4 Pediatrics and Adolescent Health

MI in pediatric settings involves a complication not present in adult encounters: the patient is a minor, and the parent or caregiver is often the primary decision-maker. This creates a "family triangle" in which the clinician must engage both the child/adolescent and the parent, sometimes with competing agendas.

Working with Parents

When the behavior-change target involves a child's behavior (diet, screen time, physical activity, medication adherence), the parent is often the person whose motivation needs to be evoked. MI with parents follows the standard template but with particular attention to autonomy support: the parent is not being told they are doing something wrong. They are being invited to explore what they want for their child and how they might achieve it.

"You've mentioned that you're worried about Maria's weight. On a 0-to-10 scale, how important is it to you to make some changes at home?" Follow-up: "Why that number and not lower?"

Working with Adolescents

Adolescents present unique motivational challenges. They are developmentally inclined toward autonomy-seeking, peer orientation, and present-focused thinking. They may be in the office because their parent brought them, not because they want to be there. MI's emphasis on autonomy support is especially critical with this population.

"I know your mom brought you in because she's worried about the vaping. I'm not here to lecture you. I'm curious about your perspective. What's your take on it?"

This opening honors the adolescent's autonomy, validates their experience of being brought to the appointment involuntarily, and invites them to share their perspective rather than defend against an accusation. If the adolescent opens up, the clinician can explore ambivalence using standard MI techniques. If the adolescent shuts down, the clinician can plant a seed and leave the door open: "It's your call. If you ever want to talk about it, I'm here."

MI for Adolescent Substance Use Prevention

Research supports brief MI for adolescent substance use prevention in primary care settings. A randomized trial found that a brief MI intervention in a primary care clinic reduced marijuana use and intentions to use among high-risk adolescents compared to usual care (D'Amico et al., 2008). The intervention was delivered in a single session and focused on exploring the adolescent's perceptions of risk and benefit, reflecting ambivalence, and evoking the adolescent's own reasons for concern.

11.5 Behavioral Health Integration

The integration of behavioral health into primary care settings has created a new clinical role: the behavioral health consultant (BHC), who provides brief (typically 15 to 30 minutes), focused interventions within the primary care workflow. MI is a natural fit for the BHC role because it is designed for brief encounters, it addresses motivation and behavior change directly, and it can be applied to the full range of conditions that BHCs encounter: depression, anxiety, substance use, chronic pain, insomnia, and chronic disease self-management.

The Warm Handoff

A warm handoff is the process by which a primary care provider introduces a patient to the BHC during the same visit. MI language can make the warm handoff more effective by framing the BHC encounter as a collaborative resource rather than a clinical referral.

MI-Inconsistent handoff: "I'm going to have you see our behavioral health person. Your depression scores are high and you need to talk to someone."

MI-Consistent handoff: "I'd like to introduce you to someone on our team who's really good at helping people figure out what's getting in the way of feeling better. They're here today, and if you're open to it, they could stop by for a few minutes."

The MI-consistent handoff preserves the patient's autonomy ("if you're open to it"), frames the BHC positively ("really good at helping people"), and avoids labeling ("your depression scores are high") that might trigger shame or resistance.

Brief MI in the 15-Minute BHC Consultation

The BHC consultation is an ideal setting for the 10-Minute MI Template. The BHC has 15 minutes, which allows for the full template plus a brief chart review and documentation. The target behavior is typically identified by the referring PCP or by the patient's presenting concern.

A BHC seeing a patient referred for difficulty managing diabetes might structure the encounter as follows:

Minutes 0 to 2: Review the referral context and engage. "Dr. Garcia mentioned that your blood sugar has been harder to manage lately. Before we dive into the numbers, I'd like to hear from you. What's been going on?"

Minutes 2 to 4: Focus on the specific behavior. "It sounds like the evenings are the hardest. That's when the snacking happens. Would it be OK if we explored that a bit?"

Minutes 4 to 10: Evoke motivation and explore barriers. Use the importance ruler, reflect change talk, offer a double-sided summary.

Minutes 10 to 13: Negotiate a micro-commitment and check confidence.

Minutes 13 to 15: Summary, affirmation, and plan for follow-up. "Would it be helpful if I checked in with you in two weeks, either by phone or at your next PCP visit?"

11.6 Case Study: Dr. Sharma and Tyler in the Emergency Department

Background

Dr. Priya Sharma encounters Tyler Briggs, a 28-year-old man, in the ED after an alcohol-related fall. BAL 0.31. Forehead lacerations. Conscious and oriented. Girlfriend just ended the relationship via text.

Presentation

Tyler is cooperative but eager to leave. He is embarrassed but not defensive. He mentions the promotion and the breakup in quick succession.

Analysis

Tyler is in a reachable moment. The combination of the acute event, the public embarrassment, and the relationship loss has temporarily disrupted his usual patterns of minimization. He is not in contemplation for sobriety, but he is emotionally open in a way he may not be tomorrow morning.

Response

Dr. Sharma does not lecture, screen, or refer. She uses the five minutes between suturing and discharge to have a human conversation.

"What was tonight supposed to look like?" (Open-ended question)

Tyler describes the promotion and the breakup. Dr. Sharma reflects: "Tonight was supposed to be a celebration, and instead it cost you something that matters a lot." (Complex reflection)

Tyler: "She said I always do this. Maybe she's right."

Dr. Sharma: "That's a big thought. What do you think she means by 'always'?" (Evocative question)

Tyler: "That every time something good happens, I drink until something bad happens."

Dr. Sharma: "You're seeing a pattern. And you're not sure what to do with it yet." (Reflection)

Tyler nods silently.

Dr. Sharma: "I'm not going to tell you what to do. That's your call. But if you ever want to talk to someone who specializes in helping people figure out their relationship with alcohol, here's a number." She writes it on a card. "No pressure. It'll be there whenever you're ready."

Outcome

Tyler took the card. Whether he called is unknown; ED follow-up data is limited. The value of the encounter cannot be measured by a single outcome. What can be measured is this: Tyler left the ED having articulated, in his own words, a pattern he had not previously named. He left with a resource he did not have before. And he left having experienced a clinical encounter that treated him as a person rather than a blood alcohol level.

Teaching Points

- The reachable moment is fleeting. Dr. Sharma used five minutes of wait time that would otherwise have been dead time.

- No commitment was sought. In the ED, seed-planting is often the most appropriate MI goal.

- The patient articulated the pattern himself ("every time something good happens, I drink until something bad happens"). This is change talk, produced organically through one well-placed evocative question.

- Providing a resource card without pressure respects autonomy and maximizes the chance that the resource will be used when the patient is ready.

11.7 Pocket Summary: Setting-Specific Adaptations

Setting	Typical Time	Primary Adaptation	Key MI Move
Emergency Department	2 to 5 min	Seed-planting during reachable moments	One reflection, one question, one resource card
Dental Practice	5 to 10 min	MI during hygiene appointment conversation time	Importance ruler for oral health; micro-commitment for home care
Pharmacy Counter	2 to 3 min	Ultra-brief E-P-E at dispensing	Elicit starting knowledge, provide in 30 seconds, elicit response
Pediatrics/Adolescents	5 to 15 min	Work with parent and/or teen	Permission-based opening with teens;

		separately; honor autonomy	parent-focused ruler for child behaviors
Behavioral Health (BHC)	15 min	Full template within consultation	Warm handoff using MI language; micro-commitment with follow-up plan

11.8 Chapter Summary

The 10-Minute MI Template is not confined to primary care or coaching offices. It adapts to any setting where behavior-change conversations occur, including emergency departments, dental practices, pharmacies, pediatric clinics, and integrated behavioral health consultations. Each setting requires specific modifications: ultra-brief seed-planting in the ED, conversation-during-cleaning in dental, two-minute E-P-E at the pharmacy counter, autonomy-centered work with adolescents, and MI-consistent warm handoffs in integrated care. The underlying principles remain the same: lead with curiosity, reflect before advising, respect autonomy, and plant seeds that may grow long after the encounter ends.

This concludes Part Three: Applied Settings and Populations. Part Four addresses the long game: teaching yourself MI, building an MI-consistent team culture, and sustaining your practice over months and years.

PART FOUR: BUILDING AND SUSTAINING MI SKILL

Chapter 12.0: Teaching Yourself MI

Dr. Nadia Petrova had read this book from cover to cover during a long weekend. She understood the spirit of MI. She could explain the OARS skills. She could recite the 10-Minute Template from memory. On Monday morning, she walked into her first patient encounter feeling prepared. The patient, a 71-year-old man with chronic obstructive pulmonary disease who continued to smoke, said: "My wife wants me to quit, but honestly, I enjoy smoking. It's the only pleasure I have left." Dr. Petrova froze. She knew she should reflect. She knew she should not argue. But in the moment, with the patient looking at her expectantly, the words that came out were: "Well, you know, smoking is really the worst thing you can do with COPD." The righting reflex had won. Knowledge, it turned out, was not the same as skill.

This chapter exists because of the gap between knowing MI and doing MI. Reading about motivational interviewing is necessary but not sufficient. MI is a performance skill, more like playing an instrument than like learning a fact. You can read a book about violin technique and understand every concept perfectly, but you will not play well until you have practiced, made mistakes, received feedback, and practiced again. The same is true for MI.

The good news is that MI skill can be developed outside of a formal multi-day training workshop. Research demonstrates that brief, skills-focused training sessions, combined with practice and feedback, can produce measurable improvements in MI competence (Schwalbe et al., 2014). The self-directed learning plan in this chapter is designed for clinicians who cannot attend a multi-day training but are committed to developing genuine MI skill through structured, deliberate practice.

By the end of this chapter, you should be able to:

1. Describe a five-phase self-directed learning arc for MI skill development.
2. Complete practice exercises for each of the four OARS skills.
3. Use the MI Self-Assessment Scorecard to evaluate your own clinical encounters.
4. Identify high-quality resources for continued MI learning.
5. Implement a 30-day learning plan that builds from reading to real-world application.

12.1 The Self-Directed Learning Arc

MI skill development follows a predictable arc. The five phases below represent a progression from passive learning to active, reflective practice. You do not need to complete one phase entirely before beginning the next; they overlap naturally. But skipping phases, particularly the practice and feedback phases, will leave significant gaps in your competence.

Phase 1: Read and Observe

This is where you are now. You have read the foundational chapters of this book and understand the concepts, skills, and template. The next step is to supplement your reading with observation. Watch MI being practiced by skilled practitioners. Video demonstrations allow you to see how the skills look and sound in real time, including the pacing, the tone of voice, the pauses, and the nonverbal communication that no written transcript can capture.

Recommended video resources include the demonstrations available through the Motivational Interviewing Network of Trainers (MINT) website, the video supplements to Miller and Rollnick's textbooks, and the free training videos available through SAMHSA (Substance Abuse and Mental Health Services Administration). When watching, pay attention to the ratio of reflections to questions, the way the practitioner responds to sustain talk, and the moments when the conversation shifts direction.

Phase 2: Practice with a Willing Partner

Before using MI with patients, practice with someone who can give you honest feedback: a colleague, a friend, or a family member. The goal is not to simulate a clinical encounter perfectly. The goal is to develop muscle memory for the core skills in a low-pressure environment.

A simple practice format: ask your partner to describe a real behavior they have been thinking about changing (exercise, diet, sleep, a habit). Then practice having a ten-minute MI conversation using the template. Afterward, ask your partner two questions: "Did you feel listened to?" and "Did I tell you what to do, or did I help you figure it out for yourself?" Their answers will be more instructive than any textbook.

Phase 3: Apply in Low-Stakes Clinical Encounters

Once you feel reasonably comfortable with the skills in practice, begin using them in real encounters. Start with low-stakes situations: a routine follow-up visit, a wellness check, a conversation about a minor lifestyle concern. Do not begin with your most complex, most resistant patient. Choose encounters where the stakes are manageable and you have a few extra minutes to be deliberate about your approach.

During this phase, you will make mistakes. You will fall into the question trap. You will accidentally give advice without using E-P-E. You will forget to reflect change talk. This is normal and expected. Each mistake is a learning opportunity, provided you notice it. The noticing is what matters.

Phase 4: Record and Self-Review

This phase is where the most significant skill growth occurs. With the patient's permission, audio-record one or two encounters per week. (Many clinics allow this with appropriate consent.) Then listen to the recording using the MI Self-Assessment Scorecard described in Section 12.3. Hearing yourself practice MI is a qualitatively different experience from remembering how you practiced. You will notice patterns you were unaware of: questions you repeat, reflections you miss, moments when the righting reflex took over without your realizing it.

If audio recording is not feasible, written self-reflection immediately after the encounter is a valuable alternative. Write down the key moments: What did the patient say? What did you say in response? What would you do differently?

Phase 5: Seek Feedback from a Peer or Coach

Self-assessment has limits. We all have blind spots. The final phase of the learning arc involves sharing your practice with someone who can offer informed feedback. This might be a colleague who is also learning MI (see Chapter 13 on peer practice groups), a clinical supervisor with MI training, or an MI trainer or coach. The Motivational Interviewing Network of Trainers (MINT) maintains a directory of trained MI practitioners and trainers worldwide who offer coaching and supervision.

Feedback is most useful when it is specific, behavioral, and constructive. "Your reflections were good" is encouraging but not instructive. "In the third minute, when the patient said she was scared of the medication, you responded with a question instead of a reflection. A reflection like 'The medication scares you' might have deepened that moment" is actionable.

12.2 Practice Exercises

The following exercises can be completed individually or with a practice partner. They are organized by OARS skill and increase in difficulty.

Open-Ended Questions: From Closed to Open

Rewrite each closed question as an open-ended question.

1. Closed: "Do you take your medication every day?" Open: "Tell me about how the medication fits into your daily routine."
2. Closed: "Are you exercising?" Open: "What role does physical activity play in your week right now?"
3. Closed: "Did you try cutting back on the drinking?" Open: "What has your experience been with your drinking since we last talked?"
4. Closed: "Is the diet working?" Open: "How have the dietary changes been going for you?"
5. Closed: "Do you want to quit smoking?" Open: "Where are you right now in your thinking about smoking?"

Practice generating your own open-ended alternatives for the closed questions you most commonly ask in your clinical setting.

Affirmations: Notice and Name

For each scenario, write an affirmation using the Notice + Name formula (notice a specific observation, name the underlying quality).

1. A patient kept all four follow-up appointments despite transportation challenges. (Example: "You found a way to get here every time, even when it was difficult. That shows real commitment.")
2. A patient honestly disclosed that they stopped taking their medication.
3. A patient tried a new exercise routine for two weeks before it fell apart.
4. A teenager admits to their parent that they have been vaping.
5. A patient with depression got out of bed and made it to today's appointment.

Reflective Listening: Simple to Complex

Read each patient statement and write three reflections: one simple, one complex (reflecting feeling or meaning), and one double-sided.

Patient statement: "I know I should eat better, but cooking takes time I don't have, and honestly, fast food just tastes good."

Simple reflection: "Fast food is convenient and you enjoy it."

Complex reflection: "There's a tension between what you know would be better for your health and what actually fits into your busy life."

Double-sided reflection: "Fast food works for your schedule and satisfies you, and at the same time, there's a part of you that wishes you were eating differently."

Practice with additional patient statements drawn from your own clinical experience.

Summaries: Building the Transitional Summary

Practice constructing a 30-second transitional summary using this template:

"So here is what I am hearing. [Two to three key points from the conversation, emphasizing change talk.] [One acknowledgment of the difficulty or ambivalence.] [A forward-looking question.]"

Example: "So here is what I am hearing. You have been thinking about your drinking for a while now, especially since your daughter said she was worried. You mentioned that you felt better during that stretch last summer when you cut back. At the same time, the evenings are hard, and the beer helps you unwind after work. Where does that leave you in terms of what you might want to do next?"

Write three transitional summaries based on recent clinical conversations, or create hypothetical scenarios for practice.

Change Talk Recognition: DARN-CAT Drill

Read each patient statement and identify the type of change talk using the DARN-CAT framework.

1. "I want to feel better when I wake up in the morning." (Desire)
2. "I've quit before, so I know I can do it again." (Ability)
3. "If I don't get this under control, I could lose my job." (Reason)
4. "Something has to change. I can't keep living like this." (Need)
5. "I'm going to call the nutritionist this week." (Commitment)
6. "I think I'm ready to try." (Activation)
7. "I actually went for a walk yesterday." (Taking steps)

Practice identifying change talk in your own clinical encounters. When you hear it, note it mentally or in the chart. Over time, your ear for change talk will become automatic.

12.3 The MI Self-Assessment Scorecard

The MI Treatment Integrity (MITI) coding system is the gold standard for evaluating MI fidelity, but it requires trained coders and is impractical for routine self-assessment (Moyers et al., 2014). The scorecard below is a simplified adaptation designed for clinicians who want to evaluate their own practice using audio recordings or detailed post-encounter notes.

How to Use the Scorecard

Listen to a recorded encounter (or review your notes immediately after) and tally each of the following behaviors.

Behavior	Tally	Target
Open-ended questions asked	___	More than closed
Closed-ended questions asked	___	Fewer than open
Simple reflections offered	___	Present but not dominant
Complex reflections offered	___	At least 40% of all reflections
Affirmations given	___	At least 1 per encounter
Summaries provided	___	At least 1, ideally transitional
Reflection-to-question ratio	___:1	Target 1:1 minimum, aim for 2:1
MI-adherent behaviors (asking permission, offering menu, emphasizing autonomy, E-P-E)	___	Present in most encounters
MI-non-adherent behaviors (advising without permission, confronting, directing, warning)	___	Minimize; aim for zero

After completing the tally, write brief answers to three reflection questions:

1. What did I do well in this encounter?
2. Where did I slip into advice-giving or the righting reflex?
3. What is one specific thing I will do differently next time?

Use the scorecard weekly during Phase 4 of the learning arc. Over time, you will see patterns: perhaps you ask too many closed questions, or your reflections are predominantly simple rather than complex, or you consistently forget to check confidence after a micro-commitment. These patterns become your personalized development targets.

12.4 Recommended Resources

Foundational Texts

Miller, W. R., & Rollnick, S. (2023). *Motivational interviewing: Helping people change and grow* (4th ed.). Guilford Press. The definitive text. Essential reading for anyone serious about MI.

Rosengren, D. B. (2018). *Building motivational interviewing skills: A practitioner workbook* (2nd ed.). Guilford Press. The best workbook available for structured skill-building with exercises, quizzes, and practice activities.

Rollnick, S., Miller, W. R., & Butler, C. C. (2008). *Motivational interviewing in health care: Helping patients change behavior*. Guilford Press. Specifically designed for healthcare settings. Shorter and more clinically focused than the core text.

Training Organizations

The Motivational Interviewing Network of Trainers (MINT) is the international professional organization for MI trainers. Their website (motivationalinterviewing.org) provides a directory of trainers, a list of upcoming workshops, and resources for learning MI. MINT membership is available to trained MI practitioners who meet specific criteria.

Online Courses and Video Resources

SAMHSA's Treatment Improvement Protocol (TIP) 35, *Enhancing Motivation for Change in Substance Use Disorder Treatment*, is freely available online and includes extensive practical guidance on MI.

Many universities and continuing education providers offer online MI courses ranging from introductory webinars to multi-week certificate programs. When evaluating courses, look for those that include live practice with feedback, not just didactic instruction.

Finding an MI Practice Group

Search the MINT directory for trainers in your area who may facilitate practice groups. Contact your local professional association (medical, nursing, social work, counseling) to ask about MI interest groups. If none exist, consider starting one using the peer practice group model described in Chapter 13.

12.5 Case Study: Dr. Petrova's 30-Day Journey

Background

Dr. Nadia Petrova, the physician from the opening vignette, recognized after her righting-reflex moment that reading the book was not enough. She committed to the 30-day self-directed learning plan.

Presentation

Week 1: Dr. Petrova re-read Chapters 3 through 5 and watched three MI demonstration videos from the MINT website. She noticed that the skilled practitioners paused more than she expected and asked far fewer questions than she would have. She practiced the closed-to-open question exercise with her spouse over dinner.

Week 2: She identified three low-stakes encounters per day and committed to using one open-ended question and one reflection in each. She caught herself giving advice without permission twice and noted both incidents in her journal.

Week 3: She began audio-recording one encounter per day (with consent). Using the Self-Assessment Scorecard, she discovered that her reflection-to-question ratio was 0.4:1, far below the 1:1 target. She was asking more than twice as many questions as she was reflecting. She set a specific goal: in every encounter, offer at least one reflection before asking the next question.

Week 4: Her reflection-to-question ratio improved to 0.8:1. She reported that conversations felt qualitatively different: patients talked more, disclosed more, and seemed more engaged. She scheduled a peer practice session with a colleague who had also read the book.

Outcome

Dr. Petrova did not become an MI expert in 30 days. Her complex reflections were still infrequent. She sometimes forgot to use E-P-E when sharing lab results. But her encounters had shifted perceptibly. Patients commented that they felt heard. Her own experience of the encounters changed: she felt less like she was pushing and more like she was listening. She described it as "less tiring, more interesting."

Teaching Points

- The gap between MI knowledge and MI skill is real and predictable. Reading is necessary but not sufficient; deliberate practice closes the gap.

- The Self-Assessment Scorecard revealed a concrete, measurable deficit (low reflection-to-question ratio) that Dr. Petrova would not have identified without data.

- Improvement was incremental, not transformative. A 30-day plan builds a foundation; sustained skill development requires ongoing practice (see Chapter 14).

- The qualitative shift in patient engagement was noticeable within weeks, reinforcing continued practice.

12.6 Pocket Summary: 30-Day MI Self-Directed Learning Plan

Week	Phase	Activities
Week 1	Read and Observe	Re-read Chapters 3 through 5. Watch 3 MI demonstration videos. Complete the closed-to-open question exercise.
Week 2	Practice with Partner and Apply	Practice the OARS exercises with a willing partner. Identify 3 low-stakes encounters daily and use one open question and one reflection in each.
Week 3	Record and Self-Review	Audio-record 1 encounter per day (with consent). Use the Self-Assessment Scorecard to evaluate each recording. Identify one specific improvement target.
Week 4	Seek Feedback and Consolidate	Share one recording with a peer or supervisor for feedback. Practice your improvement target deliberately. Schedule ongoing peer practice.

12.7 Chapter Summary

MI is a performance skill that develops through structured, deliberate practice, not through reading alone. The five-phase self-directed learning arc (read and observe, practice with a partner, apply in low-stakes encounters, record and self-review, seek feedback) provides a pathway for clinicians who cannot attend multi-day workshops. Practice exercises for each OARS skill build the foundational muscle memory. The MI Self-Assessment Scorecard provides a practical tool for tracking progress and identifying specific areas for improvement. Recommended resources, including Miller and Rollnick's core texts, the MINT network, and online training platforms, support continued development beyond the 30-day plan.

The next chapter extends MI skill development beyond the individual practitioner to the organizational level: building an MI-consistent clinic culture.

Chapter 13.0: Building an MI-Consistent Clinic Culture.

When Dr. Amara Hassan, the physician from Chapter 1, began using brief MI in her patient encounters, the results were encouraging. Her conversations felt more collaborative. Patients seemed more engaged. A few even mentioned, unprompted, that they appreciated being listened to. But Dr. Hassan quickly noticed a pattern that limited her impact. She would spend ten minutes having a carefully structured MI conversation with a patient about medication adherence, only to learn that the medical assistant had already told the patient, during the rooming process: "Dr. Hassan is going to want to talk to you about your medications. You really need to be taking them every day." The righting reflex was being activated before Dr. Hassan even entered the room.

The problem was not the medical assistant's intentions. They were excellent. The problem was that MI was operating as an individual technique in Dr. Hassan's practice rather than as a shared communication philosophy across the team. One MI-consistent clinician in an otherwise advice-driven practice is like one musician playing jazz in an orchestra performing a march. The individual performance may be skilled, but the overall experience is discordant.

This chapter addresses MI implementation at the organizational level. The evidence is clear: MI is most effective and most sustainable when it is not one practitioner's private technique but a shared practice embedded in the culture of the care team (Madson et al., 2009). Building that culture requires deliberate effort in four areas: training the whole team, creating structures for ongoing practice, integrating MI into clinical workflows, and measuring outcomes that matter.

By the end of this chapter, you should be able to:

1. Explain why individual MI skill erodes without organizational support and describe the evidence for this pattern.
2. Design an MI training approach adapted for different roles on the care team.
3. Establish a peer practice group using a structured monthly format.
4. Integrate MI documentation into the electronic health record.
5. Select meaningful outcome metrics that balance MI fidelity with patient outcomes.

13.1 From Individual Skill to Team Practice

The most consistent finding in MI implementation research is that training alone is not enough. A systematic review by Schwalbe and colleagues (2014) found that while MI training workshops produce immediate improvements in MI skill, these gains typically decay within three to six months if not supported by ongoing feedback, coaching, or structured practice. A separate review of MI implementation in substance use treatment settings found that practitioners did not consistently sustain MI after training, even when the initial training was comprehensive (Herschell et al., 2010).

The reasons for this decay are both individual and structural. At the individual level, clinicians face powerful forces pulling them back toward advice-giving: time pressure, the righting reflex, the social expectation that clinicians should "have the answers," and the lack of reinforcement for MI-consistent behavior in most clinical environments. At the structural level, most healthcare systems are designed around the biomedical model, which positions the clinician as the expert who diagnoses and prescribes. MI requires a fundamentally different relational posture, one that must be supported and reinforced by the system, not just by the individual.

The implication is practical: if you are a clinic manager, a team leader, or a change champion within your practice, your task is not simply to train individual clinicians in MI. Your task is to create an environment in which MI-consistent communication is the norm, not the exception. This requires attention to training, practice, workflow, and measurement.

> **Teaching Point:** *A useful analogy is hand hygiene. Individual clinicians know they should wash their hands. Training teaches them how. But sustained compliance requires institutional infrastructure: conveniently placed hand sanitizer, visible reminders, auditing systems, and a culture in which colleagues feel comfortable reminding each other. MI implementation follows the same logic. Individual skill matters, but sustainable practice requires organizational scaffolding.*

13.2 Training the Whole Team

MI is typically taught to clinicians: physicians, nurse practitioners, physician assistants, psychologists, social workers, counselors. But in most clinical settings, the patient's experience of the encounter begins long before they see the clinician. It begins with the phone call to schedule the appointment, the greeting at the front desk, the intake questions from the medical assistant, and the wait in the exam room. Each of these touchpoints is an opportunity to communicate in a way that is either MI-consistent (collaborative, respectful, curious) or MI-inconsistent (directive, judgmental, transactional).

Training the whole team does not mean giving everyone a full MI workshop. Different roles require different levels of training.

Front Desk and Administrative Staff

Training focus: MI spirit (CAPE), basic empathic communication, and autonomy-respectful language.

Example adaptation: Instead of "You need to fill out this form before the doctor sees you," try "I have a form I'd like you to complete when you're ready. It helps us make the most of your visit." The content is the same. The tone is collaborative rather than directive.

Duration: A 60-to-90-minute session covering the spirit of MI, the difference between directing and guiding, and specific language adaptations for scheduling, check-in, and phone interactions.

Medical Assistants and Nurses

Training focus: OARS skills (particularly open-ended questions and reflections), agenda-setting, and avoiding premature advice during rooming.

Example adaptation: During rooming, instead of "The doctor wants you to know your A1C is high and you need to lose weight," try "What would you most like to talk about with the doctor today?" This question sets the stage for the clinician's MI encounter rather than undermining it.

Duration: A half-day session (3 to 4 hours) with role-play practice. Follow-up practice sessions monthly.

Clinicians

Training focus: Full MI skill development as described in this book, including OARS, change talk recognition, the 10-Minute Template, and the Self-Assessment Scorecard.

Duration: A full-day workshop (6 to 8 hours) with role-play, video demonstration, and practice. Ongoing peer practice groups monthly.

Patient Navigators and Care Coordinators

Training focus: MI spirit, OARS skills, and the 10-Minute Template adapted for phone and in-person follow-up encounters.

Duration: A half-day session with emphasis on phone-based MI and follow-up micro-commitments. Monthly supervision.

13.3 Peer Practice Groups and Coding Circles

The most effective, lowest-cost intervention for sustaining MI skill after training is the peer practice group: a regular meeting (typically monthly, 30 to 60 minutes) in which practitioners practice MI skills together in a structured, supportive format.

Monthly Peer Practice Format (30 Minutes)

Minutes 0 to 5: Check-in. Each participant shares one MI success and one MI challenge from the past month.

Minutes 5 to 20: Skill practice. Two participants role-play a clinical encounter using the 10-Minute Template. One plays the clinician; the other plays the patient (using a realistic scenario). The rest of the group observes and takes notes.

Minutes 20 to 28: Feedback. Observers share specific, behavioral feedback using the "what worked, what to try" format. Feedback should be concrete: "When the patient said she was scared, your reflection was excellent. At the six-minute mark, you asked three questions in a row without reflecting. A reflection there might have deepened the conversation."

Minutes 28 to 30: One takeaway. Each participant identifies one specific skill they will practice before the next meeting.

The Coding Circle Variant

In a coding circle, participants bring audio recordings of actual clinical encounters (with patient consent) and review them together using the Self-Assessment Scorecard. The group tallies open vs. closed questions, counts reflections, and identifies moments of MI-adherent and MI-non-adherent behavior. This format is more intensive than role-play but produces deeper learning because it is grounded in real practice rather than simulated scenarios.

The most important ingredient in any peer practice group is psychological safety. Participants must feel that the group is a learning space, not a performance evaluation. Establishing ground rules at the outset, including confidentiality, non-judgmental feedback, and the understanding that everyone is learning, protects this safety and encourages honest self-assessment.

13.4 Workflow Integration

MI is most sustainable when it is embedded in the daily clinical workflow rather than layered on top of it. The following strategies integrate MI into the systems clinicians already use.

EHR Integration: Smart Phrases and Templates

Most electronic health record systems support smart phrases (also called dot phrases or quick text) that can be inserted into clinical notes with a few keystrokes. Create smart phrases for MI-consistent documentation:

Stage of Change documentation: "Patient appears to be in [precontemplation / contemplation / preparation / action / maintenance] regarding [target behavior]."

Ruler scores: "Importance: [X]/10. Confidence: [X]/10 for [specific behavior]."

Micro-commitment documentation: "Patient committed to [specific action] by [date/time]. Confidence level: [X]/10."

MI encounter note: "Discussed [target behavior] using MI approach. Patient expressed [change talk summary]. Agreed to [micro-commitment]. Will reassess at next visit."

These smart phrases take less than thirty seconds to insert and create a documented record that supports continuity across visits and across providers. When a colleague sees "Importance: 6/10, Confidence: 4/10 for daily walking" in the chart, they can pick up the conversation where it left off rather than starting from scratch.

Visit Preparation Checklists

A brief pre-visit checklist prompts the clinician to review the patient's MI-relevant history before the encounter:

1. What stage of change was documented at the last visit?
2. What was the micro-commitment? Was it achieved?
3. What were the importance and confidence scores?
4. What values or motivations did the patient express?

This 60-second review transforms a reactive encounter into a proactive one. The clinician enters the room already knowing the patient's motivational landscape, which allows the conversation to build on previous progress rather than repeating the same ground.

13.5 Measuring Outcomes

The temptation when implementing MI at the organizational level is to measure MI fidelity: Are clinicians using open-ended questions? Are they reflecting? Are they following the template? These process measures are important for training and quality improvement, but they are not sufficient. The ultimate question is not "Are we doing MI correctly?" but "Are our patients doing better?"

Recommended Metrics

Patient-level outcomes: A1C levels, blood pressure readings, smoking status, medication refill rates, appointment adherence, PHQ-9/GAD-7 scores. These are the outcomes that MI is designed to influence, and they should be tracked over time.

Patient experience measures: Patient satisfaction scores (CAHPS or similar), patient-reported experience of being listened to and respected, patient ratings of their involvement in care decisions.

Clinician-level process measures: Self-Assessment Scorecard results (reflection-to-question ratio, open vs. closed question balance), clinician confidence surveys (self-rated confidence in conducting MI conversations).

Organizational metrics: Percentage of encounters with documented stage of change, percentage of encounters with documented micro-commitment, frequency of peer practice group attendance.

Avoiding the Fidelity Trap

Measuring MI fidelity without measuring patient outcomes creates a perverse incentive: clinicians may learn to perform MI-adherent behaviors in ways that satisfy a coding checklist without genuinely engaging patients. A clinician who asks three open-ended questions, offers two reflections, and documents a micro-commitment has technically "done MI," but if the patient leaves feeling unheard and uncommitted, the encounter was not MI-consistent in any meaningful sense. Patient outcomes are the ultimate measure. Fidelity metrics are tools for getting there, not ends in themselves.

13.6 Case Study: The Westfield Family Medicine Transformation

Background

Westfield Family Medicine is a six-provider primary care practice serving a mixed urban-suburban population. The practice manager, Carmen Reyes, attended an MI workshop and returned with a plan to implement MI across the clinic.

Presentation

Initial attempts to implement MI by distributing this book to the clinicians produced uneven results. Two providers embraced the approach. Two read the book but did not change their practice. Two did not read the book at all. Medical assistants and front desk staff were not included in any training.

Analysis

The implementation failed because it relied on individual motivation rather than organizational structure. The providers who changed were those who were already interested in communication skills. The providers who did not change lacked the external support (training, feedback, accountability) needed to overcome the inertia of existing habits.

Response

Carmen redesigned the implementation with four components:

1. A half-day all-staff training (front desk, MAs, nurses, and providers together) focused on MI spirit and basic skills, delivered by an external MI trainer.
2. A separate full-day provider workshop with intensive role-play and Self-Assessment Scorecard introduction.
3. Monthly 30-minute peer practice sessions during the existing staff meeting time, using the structured format from Section 13.3.
4. EHR integration: smart phrases for stage of change, ruler scores, and micro-commitments were added to the visit note template.

Outcome

At six months, four of six providers were regularly using MI-consistent documentation. Peer practice attendance averaged 80 percent. Patient satisfaction scores on "feeling listened to" increased by 14 percent. A1C control rates for the diabetic population improved from 42 percent at target to 51 percent at target. The two providers who had not previously engaged both reported that the peer practice sessions were the turning point: watching colleagues practice MI made the skills feel accessible rather than theoretical.

Teaching Points

- Distributing a book is not an implementation strategy. Organizational change requires training, structure, and accountability.

- Including the entire team (not just clinicians) in MI training prevented the medical assistant from undermining the clinician's MI encounter.

- Monthly peer practice was the single most important sustaining factor, because it provided ongoing feedback, accountability, and normalization of MI as a shared team practice.

- Patient outcomes (A1C improvement, satisfaction scores) provided evidence that the investment was producing tangible results.

13.7 Pocket Summary: Clinic MI Implementation Checklist

Phase	Timeline	Key Actions
Phase 1: Foundation	Month 1	Identify a champion. Train all staff in MI spirit (half-day). Train clinicians in full MI skills (full-day).
Phase 2: Infrastructure	Month 2	Create EHR smart phrases. Establish pre-visit checklist. Schedule monthly peer practice sessions.
Phase 3: Practice and Feedback	Months 3 to 6	Conduct monthly peer practice. Collect Self-Assessment Scorecard data. Begin tracking patient outcomes.
Phase 4: Sustain and Refine	Ongoing	Maintain monthly practice. Review outcome data quarterly. Offer refresher training annually. Celebrate successes.

13.8 Chapter Summary

MI is most effective and most sustainable when it is embedded in the culture of the care team rather than practiced by isolated individuals. The evidence consistently shows that MI skills erode without ongoing support, making organizational infrastructure essential. Building an MI-consistent clinic culture requires training the whole team (not just clinicians), establishing peer practice groups for ongoing skill development, integrating MI documentation into the EHR, and measuring outcomes that include patient health indicators alongside process metrics. The implementation checklist provides a phased approach that most practices can begin within a month and sustain over time.

The final chapter addresses the long game: how to sustain your personal MI practice over months, years, and an entire career.

Chapter 14.0: Sustaining Your MI Practice Over Time.

It was a Thursday afternoon in November, and Dr. Samuel Osei, the physician we met in Chapter 8, was running 40 minutes behind. His morning had included a complicated new-patient intake, a phone call from a specialist who disagreed with his referral, and a medication authorization form that took 25 minutes to complete. His next patient was Mr. Delgado, the man with type 2 diabetes whose climbing A1C had been the focus of a productive MI conversation three months earlier. That conversation had gone well. Mr. Delgado had identified a micro-commitment, followed through, and seen his numbers improve slightly.

Today, Dr. Osei did not have the bandwidth for MI. He pulled up the labs, noted that the A1C had plateaued at 8.1, and said: "Your A1C hasn't come down much. We really need to talk about adding another medication." Mr. Delgado's expression flattened. The conversation lasted four minutes. No questions were asked. No change talk was elicited. No micro-commitment was negotiated. Dr. Osei moved to the next patient, vaguely aware that he had just done the thing he had trained himself not to do.

This chapter is about that Thursday afternoon. Not the ideal encounter. Not the demonstration case. The real one. The one where you are tired, behind schedule, emotionally depleted, and the righting reflex wins because you do not have the energy to resist it. MI skill drift is not a sign of failure. It is a predictable, well-documented phenomenon that affects every practitioner, including the most experienced. The question is not whether it will happen. The question is what you do when it does.

By the end of this chapter, you should be able to:

1. Recognize the signs and causes of MI skill drift in your own practice.
2. Describe the relationship between MI practice and clinician wellbeing.
3. Identify specific advanced MI skills to develop beyond the foundations.
4. Use a structured reflection journal to maintain self-awareness and skill.

14.1 The Skill Drift Problem

Skill drift in MI is the gradual return to pre-training communication patterns, specifically, the return to advice-giving, directive questioning, and the righting reflex. It is not a failure of character or commitment. It is a natural consequence of practicing a skill in an environment that does not consistently reinforce it.

The forces driving skill drift are powerful and pervasive. Time pressure is the most obvious. When you are behind schedule, the fastest way to address a behavior-change concern is to tell the patient what to do. A well-crafted MI conversation takes ten minutes. A directive statement takes thirty seconds. Under pressure, the brain defaults to the faster path.

The righting reflex is another force. The desire to fix, advise, and solve problems is deeply embedded in clinical training and clinical identity. Physicians, nurses, and other healthcare providers are trained to identify problems and prescribe solutions. MI asks them to do something that feels fundamentally unnatural: to sit with a patient's ambivalence without resolving it, to ask questions instead of giving answers, to let the patient lead when the clinician can see the path more clearly. This is cognitively and emotionally demanding, and when cognitive resources are depleted (as they are by mid-afternoon on a busy day), the righting reflex reasserts itself.

Social reinforcement also plays a role. Patients sometimes expect and prefer advice-giving. Colleagues may model directive communication. Organizational metrics may reward throughput over engagement. In this environment, MI-consistent behavior receives little external reinforcement, while advice-giving receives plenty.

Recognizing Your Own Drift

The first step in managing skill drift is recognizing it. The following signals suggest that drift is occurring:

You notice that you are telling patients what to do more often than asking what they want to do.

Your encounters feel more like monologues than dialogues.

Patients are giving shorter answers than they used to.

You feel frustrated by patients who "won't listen" or "won't change."

You realize you have not asked a genuine open-ended question in the last three encounters.

You catch yourself planning your response while the patient is still talking.

These signals are not cause for self-criticism. They are data. They tell you that your MI practice needs recalibration, which is a routine maintenance task, not an emergency.

Personal MI Check-In Rituals

A check-in ritual is a brief, deliberate practice that helps you reset your MI mindset during the clinical day. The following options take less than sixty seconds:

The pre-encounter pause. Before entering the exam room, take one breath and ask yourself: "What does this patient need from me? A listener or a lecturer?" The question itself shifts your posture.

The mid-day reset. At lunch, review the morning's encounters mentally. Identify one encounter where you gave advice without asking and one where you reflected well. This takes thirty seconds and recalibrates your awareness for the afternoon.

The post-encounter question. After a behavior-change encounter, ask yourself: "Did I learn something about this patient that I didn't know before?" If the answer is no, the conversation was likely clinician-driven rather than patient-centered.

14.2 MI and Clinician Wellbeing

An unexpected benefit of sustained MI practice is its effect on clinician wellbeing. This may seem counterintuitive. MI is more cognitively demanding than advice-giving. It requires deeper listening, more careful reflection, and sustained attention to the patient's language and emotions. How could it be less exhausting?

The answer lies in the nature of the exhaustion that drives clinician burnout. Research on burnout consistently identifies moral distress, the experience of knowing what should be done but feeling unable to do it, as a significant contributor (Rushton et al., 2015). In the context of behavior change, moral distress often manifests as the frustration of giving advice that patients do not follow. The clinician knows the patient needs to quit smoking, lose weight, or take their medication. They deliver the advice. The patient does not change. The clinician feels ineffective, frustrated, and eventually hopeless. This cycle, repeated across dozens of encounters per week, is deeply depleting.

MI breaks the cycle by redefining the clinician's role. In an MI framework, your job is not to make the patient change. Your job is to have a good conversation, one that is collaborative, respectful, and genuinely curious, and to create the conditions in which the patient's own motivation can emerge. The outcome of any single encounter is important, but it is not the measure of your worth or competence. A patient who leaves without a commitment has still been heard, and the relationship has been preserved for the next conversation.

This reframing does not eliminate the emotional demands of clinical work. It does, however, reduce the specific form of depletion that comes from fighting a losing battle against patient inertia. When you stop trying to push patients uphill and start walking alongside them, the work becomes lighter. Many practitioners who sustain MI over time report that their clinical encounters feel more meaningful, more human, and more energizing than the advice-giving encounters they replaced.

> **Teaching Point:** *One practitioner described the shift this way: "Before MI, I felt like every behavior-change conversation was a wrestling match. I was trying to pin the patient into compliance, and they were trying to escape. It was exhausting for both of us. With MI, I stopped wrestling. I started dancing. The patient leads, I follow, and somehow we end up somewhere better than where we started. And I'm not tired at the end of the day."*

14.3 Advanced Skill Development

Once you have established a solid foundation in the OARS skills and the 10-Minute Template, continued growth in MI involves developing more nuanced and sophisticated capabilities. The following advanced skills distinguish proficient MI practitioners from beginners.

Complex Reflections

Chapter 3 introduced complex reflections as reflections that go beyond what the patient explicitly said to capture underlying meaning, feeling, or implication. At the advanced level, complex reflections become more precise and more strategic. The practitioner learns to reflect not just what the patient is feeling but what the patient is on the verge of realizing.

Patient: "I keep putting off the appointment with the specialist. I don't know why."

Beginner reflection: "You've been procrastinating on the appointment."

Advanced reflection: "Part of you might be afraid of what the specialist will find."

The advanced reflection names an emotion (fear) that the patient has not explicitly stated but that is implied by the pattern of avoidance. If the reflection is accurate, it deepens the conversation dramatically. If it is slightly off, the patient will correct it, which is also valuable.

Strategic Use of Silence

Silence is one of the most underused tools in MI. After offering a reflection, particularly a complex one, the skilled practitioner pauses and lets the silence work. Silence gives the patient time to process what they have heard, to sit with an insight, or to formulate a response that goes deeper than their initial reaction. Many practitioners fill silence out of discomfort, but in MI, the silence after a good reflection is often the most productive moment in the encounter.

Recognizing Subtle Change Talk

Preparatory change talk is not always explicit. It may appear as a question ("How long would I need to take this medication?"), a conditional statement ("If I had more energy, I'd probably exercise"), or even a sigh followed by "I know." The advanced practitioner develops an ear for these subtle signals and reflects them: "You're starting to think about what it would take" or "Something in you is ready, even if the rest of you isn't sure yet."

When to Seek Advanced Training

If you have been practicing MI for six months or more and want to deepen your skills, consider attending an advanced MI workshop, seeking individual MI supervision or coaching from a MINT-certified trainer, or pursuing formal MI coding certification. The Motivational Interviewing Competency Assessment (MICA) and the Motivational Interviewing Treatment Integrity (MITI) coding systems provide structured frameworks for evaluating and developing advanced MI competence.

14.4 The MI Practitioner's Reflection Journal

Sustained skill development requires sustained self-awareness, and self-awareness requires a practice of reflection. The MI Practitioner's Reflection Journal is a structured journaling format designed for brief, daily or weekly use. It takes three to five minutes and consists of three questions.

Question 1: What did I hear?

Recall one encounter from the day. What did the patient say that was most important? What change talk did you notice? What sustain talk? What emotion was present beneath the surface?

This question trains your ear. Over time, you will find that your ability to recall what patients said becomes sharper and more detailed, because the act of journaling teaches you to listen more carefully during the encounter itself.

Question 2: What did I reflect?

In that same encounter, what reflections did you offer? Were they simple or complex? Did you reflect the change talk, the sustain talk, or both? Did you offer a double-sided reflection that ended on the change side? Did you miss a reflection opportunity that, in retrospect, would have deepened the conversation?

This question trains your awareness of your own in-session behavior. It helps you see the gap between what you intended to do and what you actually did.

Question 3: What would I do differently?

If you could replay the encounter, what would you change? Perhaps you asked too many questions without reflecting. Perhaps you jumped to planning before the patient was ready. Perhaps you missed a moment of change talk that, in hindsight, was the turning point the patient was offering you.

This question trains your judgment. It is not about self-criticism. It is about the deliberate, non-judgmental identification of improvement opportunities, exactly the same process MI encourages in patients.

Sample Journal Entry

"Encounter with Mrs. Rodriguez, 45, hypertension follow-up. She said her BP has been better since she started walking but she stopped last week because of back pain. I heard Ability change talk ('I know walking helps') and a barrier (back pain). I reflected the barrier but not the ability. I should have said: 'You found something that works, and now the back pain is getting in the way.' That would have honored her success and opened a conversation about how to adapt around the pain. Instead, I jumped to suggesting she try a different form of exercise, which was advice-giving. Next time: reflect the success before problem-solving the barrier."

14.5 Case Study: Dr. Osei's Thursday Recovery

Background

Dr. Samuel Osei, as described in the opening vignette, reverted to advice-giving during his encounter with Mr. Delgado on a busy Thursday afternoon.

Presentation

After the encounter, Dr. Osei felt the familiar discomfort of recognizing that he had done the thing he trained himself not to do. He had led with the lab value, suggested a medication, and ended the conversation without asking a single open-ended question.

Analysis

The drift was driven by time pressure (40 minutes behind schedule), cognitive depletion (complicated morning), and a subtle but real sense of frustration with the patient's plateaued A1C. These are the three most common drivers of skill drift: exhaustion, urgency, and outcome frustration.

Response

Dr. Osei did three things. First, he noted the drift in his Reflection Journal that evening: "Delgado encounter. I led with the A1C, suggested medication, didn't ask a single open question. Righting reflex won. I was tired and frustrated that the numbers hadn't moved more. Next time: start with 'How have things been going for you?' before touching the labs."

Second, he made a note in Mr. Delgado's chart: "Discussed A1C. Did not have time for full MI conversation today. Plan to revisit with MI approach at next visit." This documentation ensured continuity.

Third, he brought the encounter to his monthly peer practice session and used it as a role-play scenario. A colleague played Mr. Delgado, and Dr. Osei practiced the encounter again, this time leading with an open-ended question and reflecting the patient's experience before introducing the lab value. The group provided feedback: his reflection was strong, but he jumped to the ruler too quickly. A colleague suggested adding a brief exploration of what had changed since the last visit before moving to the EVOKE phase.

Outcome

At the next visit, Dr. Osei opened with: "Last time, I jumped straight into your lab results without really asking how things were going. I want to do this differently today. How have the last few weeks been for you?" Mr. Delgado's response was immediate and telling: "Honestly, my back has been killing me. I stopped walking. I know that's probably why the numbers aren't budging." The conversation that followed produced a new micro-commitment (a daily stretching routine Mr. Delgado had learned from a physical therapist years ago) and a confidence score of 8. The encounter took nine minutes.

Teaching Points

- Skill drift is recoverable. The fact that Dr. Osei reverted on Thursday does not erase his MI skills. It signals the need for recalibration, not retraining.

- The Reflection Journal provided a structured way to process the drift without self-flagellation. The entry was specific, behavioral, and forward-looking.

- Bringing the encounter to the peer practice group transformed an individual failure into a collective learning opportunity.

- The repair at the next visit, explicitly naming the previous encounter's shortcoming, actually deepened the therapeutic relationship. Mr. Delgado saw a clinician who was honest about imperfection, which modeled the same honesty MI asks of patients.

14.6 Pocket Summary: Monthly MI Skill Maintenance Calendar

Week	Activity	Time Required
Week 1	Complete 3 Reflection Journal entries (one per clinical day, choose 1 encounter each). Review your most common drift pattern.	10 to 15 min total
Week 2	Audio-record 1 encounter (with consent). Score it with the Self-Assessment Scorecard (Appendix E). Identify 1 improvement target.	20 min
Week 3	Attend monthly peer practice group or schedule a 15-min skill-swap with a colleague. Practice your improvement target in role-play.	30 min
Week 4	Review the month. Re-read 1 chapter or section of this book that addresses your	15 min

	identified challenge. Set 1 intention for next month.	

Total monthly investment: approximately 75 to 90 minutes, or less than 20 minutes per week.

14.7 Chapter Summary

MI skill drift is predictable, universal, and recoverable. It is driven by time pressure, cognitive depletion, outcome frustration, and the absence of environmental reinforcement for MI-consistent behavior. Managing drift requires not heroic willpower but practical routines: pre-encounter pauses, mid-day resets, Reflection Journal entries, and regular peer practice. Sustained MI practice also offers an unexpected benefit for clinician wellbeing by replacing the exhausting cycle of advice-giving and patient non-compliance with a collaborative approach that redefines the clinician's role and reduces moral distress.

Advanced skill development, including complex reflections, strategic silence, and subtle change talk recognition, keeps the practice fresh and deepens its impact over time. The Monthly Maintenance Calendar provides a sustainable structure for ongoing growth that requires less than 20 minutes per week.

This book began with a simple question: Is it possible to have a meaningful, evidence-based conversation about behavior change in ten minutes or less? The answer, as we have seen, is yes. But the deeper answer is that the ten-minute conversation is not a technique. It is a way of being with people, a way that respects their autonomy, trusts their capacity, and meets them wherever they are. If you practice this way of being consistently, even imperfectly, you will change the nature of your clinical relationships. And those relationships, more than any medication, any lab value, or any treatment protocol, are where healing begins.

PART FIVE: APPENDICES AND TOOLS

Appendix A: The One-Page Consult Sheet

Brief Motivational Interviewing for Busy Clinicians: The Brief MI Template

Photocopy this page. Laminate it. Tape it to your monitor. Keep it in your coat pocket.

THE 10-MINUTE MI TEMPLATE

OPEN (Minutes 0 to 2): Engage and Set the Agenda

Goal: Establish a collaborative tone. Identify what the conversation will be about.

Starter Questions:

"What matters most to you about your health right now?"

"How have things been going since we last talked?"

"There are a few things we could discuss today. Which feels most important to you?"

Permission Question (if raising a topic the patient has not mentioned):

"I noticed [clinical observation]. Would it be OK if we spent a few minutes talking about that?"

FOCUS (Minutes 2 to 4): Identify the Target Behavior

Goal: Narrow to one specific, actionable behavior. Share information using E-P-E.

Elicit-Provide-Elicit (E-P-E) Script:

Step 1 (Elicit): "What do you already know about [topic]?"

Step 2 (Provide): "Would it be helpful if I shared [brief information]?" (Keep to 2 to 3 sentences.)

Step 3 (Elicit): "What do you make of that?" or "How does that land for you?"

Link to Values:

"You mentioned [value]. How does [behavior] connect to that for you?"

EVOKE (Minutes 4 to 7): Elicit and Reinforce Change Talk

Goal: Draw out the patient's own motivation. Use rulers and evocative questions. Reflect change talk.

Importance Ruler:

"On a scale of 0 to 10, how important is it to you to [change behavior]?"

Follow-up: "Why did you say [number] and not something lower?"

Confidence Ruler:

"On the same 0-to-10 scale, how confident are you that you could do this if you decided to?"

Follow-up: "What would it take to move that number up?"

Evocative Questions:

"What would be different in your life if you made this change?"

"What are the best reasons for doing something about this?"

"What would it take for you to feel ready?"

Reflect Change Talk When You Hear It:

Patient says something that leans toward change. You reflect it back. This strengthens it.

PLAN (Minutes 7 to 10): Negotiate a Micro-Commitment

Goal: Help the patient identify one small, specific, achievable step. Check confidence. Close with affirmation.

Micro-Commitment Formula:

What will I do? + When will I do it? + Where? + How much?

Example: "I will walk around the block after dinner on Tuesday and Thursday."

Brief Action Planning Question:

"Is there anything you would be willing to do in the next week or two?"

Confidence Check:

"On a 0-to-10 scale, how confident are you that you can do this?"

If 7 or above: Affirm and close.

If below 7: "What would need to change to bring that number up?" or "Would a smaller version feel more doable?"

Closing Summary Template:

"So just to recap: [summarize what the patient said and committed to]. [Affirm the patient's strengths or effort]. I look forward to hearing how it goes."

THE 5-MINUTE EXPRESS MI VARIANT

For ultra-brief encounters when 10 minutes is not available.

Phase	Time	What to Do
OPEN	0:00 to 0:30	One warm sentence + one open-ended question
ASK	0:30 to 1:30	One evocative question or importance ruler
REFLECT + SUMMARIZE	1:30 to 3:00	Reflect change talk. Brief summary.
COMMIT	3:00 to 4:00	One micro-commitment. Confidence check.
CLOSE	4:00 to 5:00	Affirm the person and the plan.

Appendix B: The OARS Quick-Reference Card

Print double-sided. Cut to pocket size. Laminate for durability.

FRONT: THE OARS SKILLS

O: Open-Ended Questions

Invite the patient to tell their story. Cannot be answered with "yes" or "no."

"What concerns you most about your health right now?"

"How would you like things to be different?"

"Tell me about what you have already tried."

A: Affirmations

Recognize the patient's strengths, efforts, and values. Focus on the person, not just the behavior.

"You kept coming back to your appointments even when things were hard. That shows real determination."

"It took courage to be honest with me about that."

"You found a way to get started, and that takes initiative."

Formula: Notice something specific + Name the quality it reveals.

R: Reflective Listening

Offer back what the patient seems to be saying, thinking, or feeling. Use statements, not questions.

Simple reflection: "Your schedule makes it hard to eat the way you would like."

Complex reflection: "Part of you wants to change, and you are frustrated that life keeps getting in the way."

Amplified reflection: "So your drinking really has not caused any problems at all." (Invites correction.)

Double-sided reflection: "Smoking gives you something you value, and at the same time, part of you knows it is affecting your health." (End on the change side.)

Target: 2 reflections for every 1 question.

S: Summaries

Pull together what the patient has said. Three types:

Collecting: Gather several things the patient said into a bouquet.

Linking: Connect something said now to something said earlier.

Transitional: Recap the conversation, emphasize change talk, and open the door to planning. "So here is what I am hearing... Where does that leave you?"

BACK: CHANGE TALK RECOGNITION (DARN-CAT)

Preparatory Change Talk (DARN)

Type	Signal Words	Example
Desire	"I want..." "I wish..." "I would like..."	"I wish I could get my blood pressure under control."
Ability	"I could..." "I can..." "I have done it before..."	"I think I could cut back to two cigarettes a day."
Reason	"because..." "If I do not..." "It would help..."	"If I do not get this under control, I could lose my eyesight."
Need	"I have to..." "I need to..." "Something has to change..."	"Something has to change. I cannot keep going like this."

Mobilizing Change Talk (CAT)

Type	Signal Words	Example
Commitment	"I will..." "I am going to..." "I have decided..."	"I am going to call the nutritionist this week."
Activation	"I am ready..." "I am willing..." "I think the time is right..."	"I think I am ready to try."

Taking Steps	"I already..." "I started..." "I signed up..."	"I actually went for a walk yesterday."

When You Hear Change Talk: REFLECT IT.

When you hear sustain talk: Reflect it without arguing. Use straight reflection, amplified reflection, double-sided reflection, or emphasize autonomy.

Appendix C: Change Talk and Sustain Talk Recognition Guide

CHANGE TALK EXAMPLES (DARN-CAT)

Desire (D): "I want to..."

1. "I wish I had more energy to play with my kids."
2. "I would like to feel better when I wake up."
3. "I want to be healthier for my family."
4. "I hope I can get off some of these medications someday."
5. "I would love to not feel winded going up stairs."

Ability (A): "I could..."

1. "I have done it before, so I know I can do it again."
2. "I think I could manage walking a few times a week."
3. "If I really put my mind to it, I could probably cut back."
4. "I know how to cook healthy meals. I just do not do it."
5. "I was able to quit for six months last time."

Reason (R): "Because..."

1. "If I do not get my diabetes under control, I could lose my eyesight."
2. "I would save a lot of money if I quit smoking."
3. "My doctor said the medication would help with the fatigue."
4. "My blood pressure is affecting my kidneys, and that scares me."
5. "I want to be able to travel when I retire, and I cannot do that if I am this out of shape."

Need (N): "I have to..."

1. "Something has to change. I cannot keep living like this."
2. "I need to do something before it gets worse."
3. "I have to get serious about this."
4. "I must take better care of myself."

5. "I owe it to my family to get healthier."

Commitment (C): "I will..."

1. "I will call the nutritionist this week."
2. "I am going to start walking on Monday."
3. "I have decided to cut back on the drinking."
4. "I will take the medication every day this month."
5. "I am committing to checking my blood sugar daily."

Activation (A): "I am ready..."

1. "I think I am ready to make some changes."
2. "I am willing to give it a try."
3. "The time feels right."
4. "I want to take the next step."
5. "I am open to exploring this."

Taking Steps (T): "I already..."

1. "I actually went for a walk yesterday."
2. "I threw away the rest of the cigarettes."
3. "I signed up for that diabetes class."
4. "I bought a water bottle and have been carrying it to work."
5. "I told my wife I want to start eating dinner at home more."

SUSTAIN TALK EQUIVALENTS

Change Talk Category	Sustain Talk Equivalent	Example
Desire	Desire to stay the same	"I like things the way they are."
Ability	Inability to change	"I have tried before and I cannot do it."
Reason	Reasons against change	"Changing my diet would make me miserable."
Need	No perceived need	"I do not see why I need to change anything."

Commitment	Commitment to status quo	"I am not going to quit. That is final."
Activation	Unwillingness to act	"I am not ready and I do not know when I will be."
Taking Steps	Steps away from change	"I actually started smoking more since the diagnosis."

RESPONSE STRATEGIES: WHAT TO SAY WHEN YOU HEAR...

When you hear Change Talk: Reflect it. Reinforce it. Ask for more.

"It sounds like being there for your grandchildren is a powerful reason for you."

"You have done this before. What made it work that time?"

"You said you are ready. What would a first step look like?"

When you hear Sustain Talk: Do not argue. Do not correct. Use one of these:

Straight reflection: "You see your drinking as pretty manageable right now."

Amplified reflection: "There is absolutely no reason for you to change anything." (Said genuinely, not sarcastically.)

Double-sided reflection: "You enjoy the way things are, and at the same time, you are here today." (End on change side.)

Emphasize autonomy: "This is entirely your decision. No one can force you to change."

Reframe: "You have tried a dozen times, which tells me this matters enough to keep coming back to."

Appendix D: Clinical Scenario Bank

Twenty practice scenarios for skill development. Use individually or in peer practice groups. Each scenario includes a patient statement and three response options.

Scenario 1: Primary Care, Medication Adherence

Setting: Family medicine follow-up. Patient is a 58-year-old man with hypertension.

Patient statement: "I stopped taking the blood pressure pill. It makes me dizzy, and honestly, I feel fine without it."

Response A (MI-Consistent): "The dizziness made you stop, and without the medication you feel normal. What concerns you, if anything, about your blood pressure when you are not taking it?"

Why this works: Reflects the patient's experience without arguing, then uses an open-ended question to explore potential concern.

Response B (Partially MI-Consistent): "I understand the dizziness is frustrating. Let me tell you about some alternatives that might not cause that side effect."

Why this is partial: Acknowledges the concern (good) but moves to providing information without first eliciting the patient's perspective or asking permission.

Response C (MI-Inconsistent): "You really need to keep taking the medication. High blood pressure is a silent killer. You could have a stroke."

Why this fails: Uses fear-based persuasion and directive language. Activates the righting reflex. Ignores the patient's stated concern about side effects.

Scenario 2: Health Coaching, Exercise Initiation

Setting: Wellness coaching session. Client is a 34-year-old woman referred for weight management.

Patient statement: "I know I need to exercise, but I hate the gym. I went for two weeks and felt like everyone was staring at me."

Response A (MI-Consistent): "The gym felt uncomfortable, and that experience put you off. If the gym is off the table, what kind of movement might actually feel good to you?"

Response B (Partially MI-Consistent): "A lot of people feel that way at first. It gets easier once you go regularly."

Response C (MI-Inconsistent): "You just have to push through the discomfort. No one is actually looking at you."

Scenario 3: Dental, Oral Hygiene

Setting: Dental hygiene appointment. Patient is a 45-year-old man with gingivitis.

Patient statement: "I know I should floss, but I just never remember. By the time I think about it, I am already in bed."

Response A (MI-Consistent): "Flossing keeps falling off your radar at the end of the day. What do you think would make it easier to remember?"

Response B (Partially MI-Consistent): "Try keeping the floss right next to your toothbrush so you see it."

Response C (MI-Inconsistent): "You have to floss every day or the gingivitis will get worse. It only takes two minutes."

Scenario 4: Pharmacy, New Medication

Setting: Pharmacy counter. Patient is a 62-year-old woman picking up a new statin prescription.

Patient statement: "My neighbor said these cholesterol pills cause muscle pain. I am not sure I want to take it."

Response A (MI-Consistent): "Your neighbor's experience has you concerned. What would you like to know about how the medication works and what to watch for?"

Response B (Partially MI-Consistent): "Muscle pain is a possible side effect, but it only affects a small percentage of people. You should give it a try."

Response C (MI-Inconsistent): "Your neighbor is not a doctor. This medication is safe and your doctor prescribed it for a reason."

Scenario 5: Behavioral Health, Depression Treatment

Setting: Behavioral health consultation. Patient is a 29-year-old man referred for depressive symptoms.

Patient statement: "I do not think therapy works. My ex-girlfriend went for years and she was still a mess."

Response A (MI-Consistent): "Your experience watching your ex-girlfriend's therapy did not exactly inspire confidence. What would therapy need to look like for it to feel worthwhile to you?"

Response B (Partially MI-Consistent): "Everyone's experience is different. Therapy works for a lot of people."

Response C (MI-Inconsistent): "Well, you are not your ex-girlfriend. You should at least try it before deciding it does not work."

Scenario 6: Primary Care, Smoking Cessation

Setting: Annual physical. Patient is a 51-year-old woman who smokes one pack per day.

Patient statement: "I have tried quitting five times. Patches, gum, cold turkey. Nothing works for me."

Response A (MI-Consistent): "You have made five serious attempts, and each one took real effort. What have you learned from those tries about what helps and what gets in the way?"

Response B (Partially MI-Consistent): "Have you considered trying Chantix? It works differently from the patches and gum."

Response C (MI-Inconsistent): "You need to try harder. Five failed attempts means you have not found the right approach yet."

Scenario 7: Pediatrics, Adolescent Vaping

Setting: Well-child visit. Patient is a 16-year-old brought in by a parent who found a vape pen.

Patient statement: "Everyone vapes. It is not a big deal. My mom is overreacting."

Response A (MI-Consistent): "It feels like your mom is making this into something bigger than it is. I am curious, what is your take on it? What do you like about vaping?"

Response B (Partially MI-Consistent): "I understand it feels normal, but vaping does carry health risks. Would you be open to hearing about them?"

Response C (MI-Inconsistent): "Your mom is right to be worried. Vaping is addictive and it damages your lungs."

Scenario 8: Health Coaching, Nutrition

Setting: Health coaching session. Client is a 43-year-old truck driver with prediabetes.

Patient statement: "I eat what I can get on the road. There are not a lot of healthy options at truck stops."

Response A (MI-Consistent): "Your work environment makes healthy eating a real challenge. What are the options you do have access to, and are any of them ones you would actually choose?"

Response B (Partially MI-Consistent): "Some truck stops are starting to carry healthier options. You might be surprised what is available."

Response C (MI-Inconsistent): "You need to start packing your own meals. That is the only way to eat healthy on the road."

Scenario 9: Emergency Department, Alcohol-Related Injury

Setting: ED, 1:00 AM. Patient is a 25-year-old man with a fractured wrist after a fall while intoxicated.

Patient statement: "It was just a bad night. I do not usually drink this much."

Response A (MI-Consistent): "Tonight was out of the ordinary for you. What made tonight different?"

Response B (Partially MI-Consistent): "I am glad you are OK. I would recommend cutting back on the drinking to avoid injuries like this."

Response C (MI-Inconsistent): "You are in the emergency room at 1 AM with a broken wrist. This is clearly a problem."

Scenario 10: Primary Care, Diabetes Self-Management

Setting: Diabetes follow-up. Patient is a 67-year-old woman. A1C has risen from 7.2 to 8.6.

Patient statement: "I have been so busy taking care of my husband since his stroke that I have not had time to think about my own health."

Response A (MI-Consistent): "You have been pouring yourself into caring for your husband. That is a lot to carry. How has it been affecting you?"

Response B (Partially MI-Consistent): "I understand caregiving is demanding. But you need to take care of yourself too, or you will not be able to take care of him."

Response C (MI-Inconsistent): "Your A1C has gone up significantly. We need to get this under control immediately."

Scenario 11: Community Health Worker, Vaccination Hesitancy

Setting: Home visit. Client is a 38-year-old mother declining flu vaccines for her children.

Patient statement: "I do not trust vaccines. There are too many chemicals, and they give them too young."

Response A (MI-Consistent): "You are protective of your children, and you want to make sure anything that goes into their bodies is safe. What specifically concerns you most?"

Response B (Partially MI-Consistent): "I hear those concerns a lot. The ingredients in vaccines have been studied extensively and are safe."

Response C (MI-Inconsistent): "Vaccines are safe. Not vaccinating your children puts them and other kids at risk."

Scenario 12: Pharmacy, Medication Therapy Management

Setting: MTM appointment. Patient is a 72-year-old man on nine medications.

Patient statement: "I do not even know what half of these are for. I just take what the bottles say."

Response A (MI-Consistent): "That is a lot of medications to keep track of. What would be most helpful for you: understanding what each one does, or figuring out how to simplify the routine?"

Response B (Partially MI-Consistent): "Let me go through each medication and explain what it does."

Response C (MI-Inconsistent): "You should know what you are taking. Let me print out a list for you."

Scenario 13: Dental, Sugar Reduction

Setting: Dental hygiene visit. Patient is a 30-year-old woman with multiple new cavities.

Patient statement: "I know soda is bad for my teeth, but it is the only thing that gets me through the afternoon at work."

Response A (MI-Consistent): "The soda helps you power through the afternoon. If we set the teeth aside for a moment, what is it about the soda that you would miss most if you cut back?"

Response B (Partially MI-Consistent): "Have you tried switching to a sugar-free version? That would help your teeth."

Response C (MI-Inconsistent): "The soda is destroying your enamel. You need to stop drinking it."

Scenario 14: Behavioral Health, Chronic Pain

Setting: BHC consultation. Patient is a 55-year-old woman with chronic low back pain requesting increased opioid dosage.

Patient statement: "The pills are the only thing that helps. I cannot function without them."

Response A (MI-Consistent): "The medication has been the one thing that gives you relief. What does a day without pain look like for you? What are you able to do?"

Response B (Partially MI-Consistent): "I understand the medication helps. There are also some non-medication approaches that can work alongside it. Would you be open to hearing about them?"

Response C (MI-Inconsistent): "We cannot keep increasing the dose. You need to try physical therapy instead."

Scenario 15: Health Coaching, Sleep

Setting: Coaching session. Client is a 41-year-old executive sleeping 4 to 5 hours per night.

Patient statement: "Sleep is a luxury I cannot afford right now. I will sleep when things calm down."

Response A (MI-Consistent): "Right now, work takes priority over sleep. What would need to change for sleep to move up your list?"

Response B (Partially MI-Consistent): "Sleep deprivation actually makes you less productive. You might get more done if you slept more."

Response C (MI-Inconsistent): "That attitude is going to catch up with you. You need at least seven hours."

Scenario 16: Primary Care, Alcohol Reduction

Setting: Annual physical. Patient is a 48-year-old man. AUDIT score is 12.

Patient statement: "I only drink on weekends, and it is all social. I do not have a problem."

Response A (MI-Consistent): "Your drinking feels social and contained to the weekends. I am curious, what does a typical weekend look like in terms of how much you drink?"

Response B (Partially MI-Consistent): "Weekend drinking can still add up. Your screening score suggests it might be more than you realize."

Response C (MI-Inconsistent): "Your AUDIT score is 12, which puts you in the hazardous range. You are drinking too much."

Scenario 17: Pediatrics, Childhood Obesity (Parent Conversation)

Setting: Well-child visit. Parent of a 10-year-old with a BMI in the 95th percentile.

Parent statement: "He is just a big kid. My whole family is big. It is genetics."

Response A (MI-Consistent): "Your family's build is part of who he is. What concerns you, if anything, about his health as he grows?"

Response B (Partially MI-Consistent): "Genetics do play a role, but lifestyle factors matter too. There are things we can do."

Response C (MI-Inconsistent): "His weight puts him at risk for diabetes and heart disease. We need to put him on a diet."

Scenario 18: Urgent Care, Stress-Related Visit

Setting: Urgent care. Patient is a 37-year-old teacher presenting with headaches and insomnia.

Patient statement: "I just need something for the headaches. I do not have time for anything else."

Response A (MI-Consistent): "You are here for the headaches, and that is what we will address. I am also noticing you mentioned not sleeping well. Would it be all right if I asked you a couple of questions about that?"

Response B (Partially MI-Consistent): "The headaches might be connected to your sleep. Let me prescribe something for both."

Response C (MI-Inconsistent): "Your headaches are probably from stress and poor sleep. You need to make lifestyle changes."

Scenario 19: Integrated Care, Warm Handoff

Setting: Primary care. PCP introducing patient to the behavioral health consultant.

Patient statement (from PCP to patient): Patient has a PHQ-9 of 14 and is reluctant to see "a therapist."

Response A (MI-Consistent PCP handoff): "I would like to introduce you to someone on our team who is really good at helping people figure out what is getting in the way of feeling better. They are here today. Would you be open to meeting them for a few minutes?"

Response B (Partially MI-Consistent): "I would like you to see our behavioral health consultant. Your depression scores are elevated and they can help."

Response C (MI-Inconsistent): "Your depression is getting worse. I am going to have you see our therapist today."

Scenario 20: Community Health Worker, Chronic Disease Follow-Up

Setting: Phone follow-up. Client is a 60-year-old woman with heart failure who missed her last two cardiology appointments.

Patient statement: "I just do not see the point. The doctor says the same thing every time, and nothing changes."

Response A (MI-Consistent): "The appointments have not felt useful to you. What would make a visit to the cardiologist feel worth your time?"

Response B (Partially MI-Consistent): "I understand it feels repetitive. But these visits help us catch problems early."

Response C (MI-Inconsistent): "Missing your appointments is dangerous. You have heart failure and you need to be monitored."

Appendix E: The MI Self-Assessment Scorecard

Use this scorecard to evaluate your own clinical encounters. Complete it after listening to an audio recording or immediately after an encounter from memory. Track your scores over time to identify patterns and improvement targets.

ENCOUNTER INFORMATION

Date: ______________

Patient initials or identifier: ______________

Setting: ______________

Target behavior discussed: ______________

Approximate length of MI portion of encounter: ______________ minutes

SKILL TALLIES

Place a tally mark for each occurrence during the encounter.

Questions

Skill	Tally	Count
Open-ended questions		
Closed-ended questions		

Ratio: Open-ended / Closed-ended = _____ : _____

Target: More open-ended than closed-ended.

Reflections

Skill	Tally	Count
Simple reflections (repeating or rephrasing)		
Complex reflections (reflecting meaning, feeling, or the unstated)		

Total reflections: _____

Percentage complex: _____ %

Target: At least 40% complex reflections.

Reflection-to-Question Ratio

Total reflections: _____ divided by **Total questions:** _____ = _____ : 1

Target: 1:1 minimum. Aim for 2:1.

Affirmations

Skill	Tally	Count
Affirmations given (specific, genuine, person-focused)		

Target: At least 1 per encounter.

Summaries

Skill	Tally	Count
Collecting summaries		
Linking summaries		
Transitional summaries		

Target: At least 1 summary per encounter. Ideally 1 transitional summary near the end.

MI-ADHERENT BEHAVIORS

Check each behavior you demonstrated during the encounter.

Behavior	Present?
Asked permission before raising a topic or sharing information	

Used Elicit-Provide-Elicit when sharing clinical information	
Offered a menu of options rather than a single directive	
Emphasized patient autonomy ("It is your decision")	
Reflected change talk when it appeared	
Used the importance or confidence ruler	
Negotiated a micro-commitment collaboratively	
Checked confidence on the micro-commitment	
Closed with an affirmation	

MI-NON-ADHERENT BEHAVIORS

Check any behavior you demonstrated during the encounter. The goal is to minimize these.

Behavior	Present?
Advised without permission	
Confronted the patient about their behavior	
Directed the patient to do something specific without collaboration	
Warned about consequences without exploring the patient's perspective	
Argued against the patient's sustain talk	
Provided more than 3 sentences of information without returning to the patient	

REFLECTION NOTES

1. What did I do well in this encounter?

____

____

2. Where did I slip into advice-giving or the righting reflex?

____

____

3. What is one specific thing I will do differently next time?

____

____

TRACKING YOUR PROGRESS

Record your Reflection-to-Question ratio weekly. Plot it over time to visualize improvement.

Week	Reflection-to-Question Ratio	Key Observation
Week 1	: 1	
Week 2	: 1	
Week 3	: 1	
Week 4	: 1	
Week 5	: 1	
Week 6	: 1	
Week 7	: 1	
Week 8	: 1	

Appendix F: Elicit-Provide-Elicit Scripts for Common Topics

Pre-built E-P-E scripts for nine common clinical conversations. Adapt the language to fit your setting, your patient population, and your own voice.

Script 1: Medication Adherence

Elicit: "What has your experience been with [medication name]? How has it been fitting into your routine?"

Provide (with permission): "Would it be all right if I shared something about how this medication works? [Wait for yes.] This medication works gradually over weeks and months. You may not feel a difference day to day, but it is working to protect your [organ/system] over time."

Elicit: "Knowing that, what are your thoughts about giving it a consistent try?"

Script 2: Smoking Cessation

Elicit: "Where are you right now in your thinking about smoking? Is it something you have been considering changing, or is it not on your radar?"

Provide (with permission): "Would it be helpful if I mentioned one thing? [Wait.] There are now several options beyond willpower alone. Medications, nicotine replacement, and support programs can double or triple the chances of quitting successfully."

Elicit: "What stands out to you from that? Is there anything that sounds worth exploring?"

Script 3: Alcohol Reduction

Elicit: "Tell me about your relationship with alcohol. What role does it play in your life?"

Provide (with permission): "I appreciate you sharing that. Would it be OK if I shared what the screening questionnaire suggested? [Wait.] The scores indicate that your pattern of drinking may be putting some additional strain on your health, particularly your liver and blood pressure."

Elicit: "What is your reaction to hearing that?"

Script 4: Physical Activity

Elicit: "What kind of movement or activity have you enjoyed in the past, even if it has been a while?"

Provide (with permission): "Can I share one thing that surprises a lot of people? [Wait.] Even ten minutes of walking per day has measurable health benefits. You do not need to join a gym or run a marathon to get a meaningful return."

Elicit: "Knowing that, what kind of movement feels realistic for your life right now?"

Script 5: Nutrition

Elicit: "Tell me about how eating works in your day. What does a typical day look like?"

Provide (with permission): "Would it be helpful if I shared one specific thing that tends to make a noticeable difference? [Wait.] For many people, the single biggest change is replacing one processed meal per day with something prepared at home, even something simple."

Elicit: "Does that seem realistic for your situation, or would something different fit better?"

Script 6: Sleep Hygiene

Elicit: "How has your sleep been? What does a typical night look like from the time you get into bed to when you fall asleep?"

Provide (with permission): "Would you like to hear one thing that often makes a difference? [Wait.] Most sleep specialists recommend a consistent bedtime and wake time, even on weekends. The consistency trains the body's internal clock."

Elicit: "What do you think about trying that? What would get in the way?"

Script 7: Vaccination Hesitancy

Elicit: "What are your thoughts about the [specific vaccine]? What have you heard, and what concerns you?"

Provide (with permission): "Thank you for sharing that. Would it be all right if I addressed the [specific concern] directly? [Wait.] [Provide brief, factual, 2-sentence response addressing the stated concern.]"

Elicit: "How does that information affect your thinking? Where does it leave you?"

Script 8: Chronic Pain Self-Management

Elicit: "Tell me about what your pain management looks like right now. What are you doing to manage it, and how well is it working?"

Provide (with permission): "There are a few approaches that research shows can help alongside medication: specific exercises, pacing activities through the day, and techniques for managing the stress that often makes pain worse. Would you like to hear about any of these?"

Elicit: "Of those, what sounds like it might be worth trying? Or is there something else you have been curious about?"

Script 9: Mental Health Treatment Engagement

Elicit: "What has your experience with counseling or therapy been in the past, if any? What worked and what did not?"

Provide (with permission): "Would it be helpful if I described what therapy looks like here, since it may be different from what you have experienced? [Wait.] Our approach is collaborative. You set the agenda. The therapist helps you figure out what is getting in the way and how to move forward. It is not about lying on a couch."

Elicit: "How does that compare to what you were expecting? Is that something you would be open to trying?"

Appendix G: The 5-Minute Express MI Card

Print this card for ultra-brief encounters. Cut to pocket size. Laminate for durability.

EXPRESS MI: THE 5-MINUTE TEMPLATE

For encounters when 10 minutes is not available.

OPEN (0:00 to 0:30)

One warm sentence. One open-ended question.

"Good to see you. What is most important to you health-wise right now?"

ASK (0:30 to 1:30)

One strong evocative question or one importance ruler.

"On a 0-to-10 scale, how important is it to you to [behavior]?"

Follow-up: "Why that number and not lower?"

REFLECT + SUMMARIZE (1:30 to 3:00)

Reflect the change talk you heard. Offer a brief summary.

"So you are concerned about [X], and you can see that [change] could help with that."

COMMIT (3:00 to 4:00)

One micro-commitment. One confidence check.

"Is there one small thing you would be willing to try before our next visit?"

"How confident are you, 0 to 10, that you can do that?"

If below 7: "What would make it more doable?"

CLOSE (4:00 to 5:00)

Affirm the person. Affirm the plan.

"You identified something concrete, and that takes initiative. I will check in on how it goes."

Remember: A 5-minute MI conversation that plants a seed is infinitely better than a 5-minute lecture that activates the righting reflex.

Appendix H: Recommended Reading and Resources

Foundational Texts

Miller, W. R., & Rollnick, S. (2023). *Motivational interviewing: Helping people change and grow* (4th ed.). Guilford Press.

The definitive text on MI theory and practice, now in its fourth edition. Essential reading for any serious MI practitioner. The most current and comprehensive treatment of the method by its creators.

Miller, W. R., & Rollnick, S. (2013). *Motivational interviewing: Helping people change* (3rd ed.). Guilford Press.

The third edition remains widely cited and is often the version referenced in clinical training programs. Available at lower cost than the fourth edition and still highly relevant.

Rollnick, S., Miller, W. R., & Butler, C. C. (2008). *Motivational interviewing in health care: Helping patients change behavior.* Guilford Press.

A shorter, more clinically focused text specifically designed for healthcare settings. Excellent for clinicians who want MI skills without the full theoretical depth of the core text.

Rosengren, D. B. (2018). *Building motivational interviewing skills: A practitioner workbook* (2nd ed.). Guilford Press.

The best available workbook for structured MI skill development. Includes exercises, quizzes, role-play scenarios, and self-assessment tools. Highly recommended as a companion to this book.

Applications of MI Series (Guilford Press)

The "Applications of Motivational Interviewing" series, edited by Stephen Rollnick, William R. Miller, and Theresa B. Moyers, includes specialized volumes for different populations and settings:

Arkowitz, H., Miller, W. R., & Rollnick, S. (Eds.). (2015). *Motivational interviewing in the treatment of psychological problems* (2nd ed.). Guilford Press.

Naar, S., & Safren, S. A. (2017). *Motivational interviewing and CBT: Combining strategies for maximum effectiveness.* Guilford Press.

Lanier, C. H., Harlow, J. W., & Simmons, L. A. (2024). *Motivational interviewing in life and health coaching: A guide to effective practice.* Guilford Press.

Training Organizations

Motivational Interviewing Network of Trainers (MINT)

Website: motivationalinterviewing.org

The international professional organization for MI trainers. Provides a trainer directory, workshop listings, learning resources, and membership for trained MI practitioners. MINT membership requires completion of a Training New Trainers (TNT) event.

Substance Abuse and Mental Health Services Administration (SAMHSA)

SAMHSA's Treatment Improvement Protocol (TIP) 35, *Enhancing Motivation for Change in Substance Use Disorder Treatment* (updated 2019), is freely available online and includes extensive practical guidance on MI, including clinical examples, exercises, and implementation strategies. Available at: https://store.samhsa.gov

Brief Action Planning

Cole, S., Davis, C., Cole, M., & Gutnick, D. (2019). Motivational interviewing and the patient-centered medical home: A strategic approach to self-management support in primary care. *Patient Education and Counseling*, 102(2), 212-219.

The foundational article on Brief Action Planning (BAP), the streamlined planning tool referenced in Chapter 5 of this book.

Centre for Collaboration, Motivation and Innovation (CCMI)

Website: centrecmi.ca

Provides free resources, training materials, and videos on Brief Action Planning.

Key Systematic Reviews and Meta-Analyses

Frost, H., et al. (2018). Effectiveness of motivational interviewing on adult behaviour change in health and social care settings: A systematic review of reviews. *PLOS ONE*, 13(10), e0204890.

The most comprehensive recent review of MI effectiveness, covering 17 systematic reviews across health and social care.

Lundahl, B. W., et al. (2010). A meta-analysis of motivational interviewing: Twenty-five years of empirical studies. *Research on Social Work Practice*, 20(2), 137-160.

The landmark meta-analysis of 119 studies demonstrating MI's effectiveness across populations and settings.

Palacio, A., et al. (2016). Motivational interviewing improves medication adherence: A systematic review and meta-analysis. *Journal of General Internal Medicine*, 31(8), 929-940.

Focused review on MI and medication adherence, directly relevant to primary care practice.

Schwalbe, C. S., Oh, H. Y., & Zweben, A. (2014). Sustaining motivational interviewing: A meta-analysis of training studies. *Addiction*, 109(8), 1287-1294.

Critical reading on why MI skills decay after training and what sustains them, directly relevant to Chapters 12 through 14 of this book.

Magill, M., et al. (2018). A meta-analysis of motivational interviewing process: Technical, relational, and conditional process models of change. *Journal of Consulting and Clinical Psychology*, 86(2), 140-157.

The most rigorous examination of how MI works at the process level, including the relationship between clinician behavior and patient change talk.

MI Fidelity and Coding

Moyers, T. B., Manuel, J. K., & Ernst, D. (2014). *Motivational interviewing treatment integrity coding manual 4.2.1.* Unpublished manual. University of New Mexico Center on Alcoholism, Substance Abuse, and Addictions.

The gold standard for MI fidelity assessment. Available through the MINT network and the University of New Mexico CASAA website.

Appendix I: Glossary of MI Terms

Affirmation. A statement that recognizes a patient's strengths, efforts, values, or qualities. Distinct from praise, which evaluates behavior. Example: "You showed real determination in coming back to this appointment."

Ambivalence. The simultaneous experience of wanting to change and wanting to stay the same. A normal part of the change process, not a pathological state. MI is specifically designed to help people explore and resolve ambivalence.

Autonomy support. The practice of explicitly recognizing the patient's right to make their own decisions, even when the clinician disagrees with those decisions. A core component of MI spirit.

Brief Action Planning (BAP). A streamlined planning tool developed by Steven Cole and colleagues for use in time-constrained settings. Integrates with the PLAN phase of the 10-Minute MI Template.

CAPE. An acronym for the four elements of MI spirit: Compassion, Acceptance, Partnership, and Evocation (or Empowerment).

Change talk. Any patient language that favors movement toward change. Organized by the DARN-CAT framework. The amount and strength of change talk during a session predicts subsequent behavior change.

Closed-ended question. A question that can be answered with a single word or brief factual response (e.g., "Do you smoke?"). Useful for gathering specific information but limits exploration.

Collecting summary. A type of summary that gathers together several things the patient has said during the conversation.

Complex reflection. A reflection that goes beyond what the patient explicitly said to reflect underlying meaning, feeling, or implication.

Confidence ruler. A 0-to-10 scale used to assess how confident a patient feels about their ability to make a specific change. Used alongside the importance ruler.

DARN-CAT. A mnemonic for the seven categories of change talk: Desire, Ability, Reason, Need (preparatory change talk) and Commitment, Activation, Taking steps (mobilizing change talk).

Discord. A strain in the therapeutic relationship, signaled by arguing, interrupting, disengaging, or ignoring. Distinct from sustain talk, which is about the behavior rather than the relationship.

Double-sided reflection. A reflection that captures both sides of the patient's ambivalence in a single statement, typically ending on the change side. Uses "and" rather than "but."

Elicit-Provide-Elicit (E-P-E). A three-step structure for sharing information in an MI-consistent way. Step 1: Elicit what the patient knows or wants to know. Step 2: Provide information briefly and with permission. Step 3: Elicit the patient's response.

Engaging. The first of MI's four processes. The process of establishing a mutually trusting and respectful working relationship.

Evoking. The third of MI's four processes. The strategic, skillful process of drawing out the patient's own motivations for change. The heart of MI.

Focusing. The second of MI's four processes. The process of developing and maintaining a specific direction in the conversation.

Importance ruler. A 0-to-10 scale used to assess how important a specific behavior change is to the patient. The follow-up question ("Why that number and not lower?") is designed to elicit change talk.

Linking summary. A type of summary that connects something the patient said now to something they said earlier in the conversation or in a previous visit.

Micro-commitment. A small, specific, measurable, and achievable action step that the patient identifies and agrees to take before the next contact. The output of the PLAN phase.

MI-adherent behavior. Clinician behavior that is consistent with MI principles, including asking permission, emphasizing autonomy, offering a menu of options, and using E-P-E.

MI-non-adherent behavior. Clinician behavior that is inconsistent with MI principles, including advising without permission, confronting, directing, and warning.

MI spirit. The foundational attitude underlying all MI practice, encompassing Compassion, Acceptance, Partnership, and Evocation (CAPE). More important than any individual technique.

Mobilizing change talk. The stronger form of change talk that signals movement from contemplation toward action. Includes Commitment, Activation, and Taking Steps (the CAT in DARN-CAT).

OARS. An acronym for the four core communication skills of MI: Open-ended questions, Affirmations, Reflective listening, and Summaries.

Open-ended question. A question that invites the patient to think, reflect, and elaborate, and that cannot be answered with a single word. Example: "How would you like things to be different?"

Planning. The fourth of MI's four processes. The process of supporting the patient in developing a concrete plan for change when they are ready. Optional; not every encounter will reach this process.

Preparatory change talk. Change talk that signals consideration of change but not yet commitment to it. Includes Desire, Ability, Reason, and Need (the DARN in DARN-CAT).

Reflective listening. The practice of offering back to the patient what they seem to be saying, thinking, or feeling. A statement, not a question. The most important and most difficult MI skill.

Righting reflex. The natural human impulse to fix what appears broken. In clinical settings, it manifests as the urge to advise, correct, or persuade. When left unchecked, it often produces the opposite of the intended effect by activating the patient's defense of the status quo.

Simple reflection. A reflection that repeats or slightly rephrases what the patient said, without adding new meaning or interpretation.

Stages of Change (Transtheoretical Model). A model of behavior change developed by James Prochaska and Carlo DiClemente, describing five stages: precontemplation, contemplation, preparation, action, and maintenance. MI was specifically designed to work with the contemplation stage but adapts to all stages.

Sustain talk. Any patient language that favors maintaining the status quo. The opposite of change talk. A normal expression of ambivalence, not a pathology to be defeated. Responding to sustain talk without arguing against it is a core MI skill.

Transitional summary. A type of summary used to signal a shift in the conversation, typically from the evoking process to the planning process. Recaps the conversation, emphasizes change talk, and opens the door to next steps.

Transtheoretical Model (TTM). See Stages of Change.

References

Academic ED SBIRT Research Collaborative. (2007). The impact of screening, brief intervention, and referral for treatment on emergency department patients' alcohol use. *Annals of Emergency Medicine, 50*(6), 699–710.

Amrhein, P. C., Miller, W. R., Yahne, C. E., Palmer, M., & Fulcher, L. (2003). Client commitment language during motivational interviewing predicts drug use outcomes. *Journal of Consulting and Clinical Psychology, 71*(5), 862–878.

Bernstein, J., Heeren, T., Edward, E., Dorfman, D., Bliss, C., Winter, M., & Bernstein, E. (2010). A brief motivational interview in a pediatric emergency department, plus 10-day telephone follow-up, increases attempts to quit drinking among youth and young adults who screen positive for problematic drinking. *Academic Emergency Medicine, 17*(8), 890–902.

Cascaes, A. M., Bielemann, R. M., Clark, V. L., & Barros, A. J. D. (2014). Effectiveness of motivational interviewing at improving oral health: A systematic review. *Revista de Saúde Pública, 48*(1), 142–153.

Cole, S., Davis, C., Cole, M., & Gutnick, D. (2010). Motivational interviewing and the patient centered medical home: A strategic approach to self-management support in primary care. In *Health IT in the patient centered medical home*. Patient-Centered Primary Care Collaborative.

D'Amico, E. J., Miles, J. N. V., Stern, S. A., & Meredith, L. S. (2008). Brief motivational interviewing for teens at risk of substance use consequences: A randomized pilot study in a primary care clinic. *Journal of Substance Abuse Treatment, 35*(1), 53–61.

Fiore, M. C., Jaén, C. R., Baker, T. B., Bailey, W. C., Benowitz, N. L., Curry, S. J., Dorfman, S. F., Froelicher, E. S., Goldstein, M. G., Healton, C. G., Henderson, P. N., Heyman, R. B., Koh, H. K., Kottke, T. E., Lando, H. A., Mecklenburg, R. E., Mermelstein, R. J., Mullen, P. D., Orleans, C. T., … Wewers, M. E. (2008). *Treating tobacco use and dependence: 2008 update*. U.S. Department of Health and Human Services, Public Health Service.

Frost, H., Campbell, P., Maxwell, M., O'Carroll, R. E., Dombrowski, S. U., Williams, B., Cheyne, H., Coles, E., & Pollock, A. (2018). Effectiveness of motivational interviewing on adult behaviour change in health and social care settings: A systematic review of reviews. *PLOS ONE, 13*(10), Article e0204890.

Gollwitzer, P. M. (1999). Implementation intentions: Strong effects of simple plans. *American Psychologist, 54*(7), 493–503.

Herschell, A. D., Kolko, D. J., Baumann, B. L., & Davis, A. C. (2010). The role of therapist training in the implementation of psychosocial treatments: A review and critique with recommendations. *Clinical Psychology Review, 30*(4), 448–466.

Hettema, J., Steele, J., & Miller, W. R. (2005). Motivational interviewing. *Annual Review of Clinical Psychology, 1*, 91–111.

Knowler, W. C., Barrett-Connor, E., Fowler, S. E., Hamman, R. F., Lachin, J. M., Walker, E. A., & Nathan, D. M. (2002). Reduction in the incidence of type 2 diabetes with lifestyle intervention or metformin. *The New England Journal of Medicine, 346*(6), 393–403.

Lundahl, B. W., Kunz, C., Brownell, C., Tollefson, D., & Burke, B. L. (2010). A meta-analysis of motivational interviewing: Twenty-five years of empirical studies. *Research on Social Work Practice, 20*(2), 137–160.

Madson, M. B., Loignon, A. C., & Lane, C. (2009). Training in motivational interviewing: A systematic review. *Journal of Substance Abuse Treatment, 36*(1), 101–109.

Magill, M., Apodaca, T. R., Borsari, B., Gaume, J., Hoadley, A., Gordon, R. E. F., Tonigan, J. S., & Moyers, T. B. (2018). A meta-analysis of motivational interviewing process: Technical, relational, and conditional process models of change. *Journal of Consulting and Clinical Psychology, 86*(2), 140–157.

Magill, M., Gaume, J., Apodaca, T. R., Walthers, J., Mastroleo, N. R., Borsari, B., & Longabaugh, R. (2014). The technical hypothesis of motivational interviewing: A meta-analysis of MI's key causal model. *Journal of Consulting and Clinical Psychology, 82*(6), 973–983.

Martins, R. K., & McNeil, D. W. (2009). Review of motivational interviewing in promoting health behaviors. *Clinical Psychology Review, 29*(4), 283–293.

Miller, W. R. (1983). Motivational interviewing with problem drinkers. *Behavioural Psychotherapy, 11*(2), 147–172.

Miller, W. R., & Rollnick, S. (2013). *Motivational interviewing: Helping people change* (3rd ed.). Guilford Press.

Miller, W. R., & Rollnick, S. (2023). *Motivational interviewing: Helping people change and grow* (4th ed.). Guilford Press.

Miller, W. R., & Rose, G. S. (2009). Toward a theory of motivational interviewing. *American Psychologist, 64*(6), 527–537.

Moyer, A., Finney, J. W., Swearingen, C. E., & Vergun, P. (2002). Brief interventions for alcohol problems: A meta-analytic review of controlled investigations in treatment-seeking and non-treatment-seeking populations. *Addiction, 97*(3), 279–292.

Moyers, T. B., Manuel, J. K., & Ernst, D. (2015). *Motivational interviewing treatment integrity coding manual 4.2.1* [Unpublished manual]. Center on Alcoholism, Substance Abuse and Addictions, University of New Mexico.

Moyers, T. B., Martin, T., Houck, J. M., Christopher, P. J., & Tonigan, J. S. (2009). From in-session behaviors to drinking outcomes: A causal chain for motivational interviewing. *Journal of Consulting and Clinical Psychology, 77*(6), 1113–1124.

Moyers, T. B., Martin, T., Manuel, J. K., Hendrickson, S. M. L., & Miller, W. R. (2005). Assessing competence in the use of motivational interviewing. *Journal of Substance Abuse Treatment, 28*(1), 19–26.

Palacio, A., Garay, D., Langer, B., Taylor, J., Wood, B. A., & Tamariz, L. (2016). Motivational interviewing improves medication adherence: A systematic review and meta-analysis. *Journal of General Internal Medicine, 31*(8), 929–940.

Pollak, K. I., Alexander, S. C., Tulsky, J. A., Lyna, P., Coffman, C. J., Dolor, R. J., Gulbrandsen, P., & Østbye, T. (2011). Physician empathy and listening: Associations with patient satisfaction and autonomy. *Journal of the American Board of Family Medicine, 24*(6), 665–672.

Prochaska, J. O., & DiClemente, C. C. (1983). Stages and processes of self-change of smoking: Toward an integrative model of change. *Journal of Consulting and Clinical Psychology, 51*(3), 390–395.

Prochaska, J. O., DiClemente, C. C., & Norcross, J. C. (1992). In search of how people change: Applications to addictive behaviors. *American Psychologist, 47*(9), 1102–1114.

Rollnick, S., Miller, W. R., & Butler, C. C. (2008). *Motivational interviewing in health care: Helping patients change behavior*. Guilford Press.

Rosengren, D. B. (2018). *Building motivational interviewing skills: A practitioner workbook* (2nd ed.). Guilford Press.

Rubak, S., Sandbæk, A., Lauritzen, T., & Christensen, B. (2005). Motivational interviewing: A systematic review and meta-analysis. *British Journal of General Practice, 55*(513), 305–312.

Rushton, C. H., Batcheller, J., Schroeder, K., & Donohue, P. (2015). Burnout and resilience among nurses practicing in high-intensity settings. *American Journal of Critical Care, 24*(5), 412–420.

Sabaté, E. (Ed.). (2003). *Adherence to long-term therapies: Evidence for action*. World Health Organization.

Saitz, R., Palfai, T. P. A., Cheng, D. M., Alford, D. P., Bernstein, J. A., Lloyd-Travaglini, C. A., Meli, S. M., Chaisson, C. E., & Samet, J. H. (2014). Screening and brief intervention for drug use in primary care: The ASPIRE randomized clinical trial. *JAMA, 312*(5), 502–513.

Schwalbe, C. S., Oh, H. Y., & Zweben, A. (2014). Sustaining motivational interviewing: A meta-analysis of training studies. *Addiction, 109*(8), 1287–1294.

Simmons, L. A., & Wolever, R. Q. (2013). Integrative health coaching and motivational interviewing: Synergistic approaches to behavior change in healthcare. *Global Advances in Health and Medicine, 2*(4), 28–35.

Tai-Seale, M., McGuire, T. G., & Zhang, W. (2007). Time allocation in primary care office visits. *Health Services Research, 42*(5), 1871–1894.

Thompson, D. R., Chair, S. Y., Chan, S. W., Astin, F., Davidson, P. M., & Ski, C. F. (2011). Motivational interviewing: A useful approach to improving cardiovascular health? *Journal of Clinical Nursing, 20*(9–10), 1236–1244.

Viswanathan, M., Golin, C. E., Jones, C. D., Ashok, M., Blalock, S. J., Wines, R. C. M., Coker-Schwimmer, E. J. L., Rosen, D. L., Sista, P., & Lohr, K. N. (2012). Interventions to improve adherence to self-administered medications for chronic diseases in the United States: A systematic review. *Annals of Internal Medicine, 157*(11), 785–795.

Walker, M. (2017). *Why we sleep: Unlocking the power of sleep and dreams*. Scribner.

Yarnall, K. S. H., Pollak, K. I., Østbye, T., Krause, K. M., & Michener, J. L. (2003). Primary care: Is there enough time for prevention? *American Journal of Public Health, 93*(4), 635–641.

Yevlahova, D., & Satur, J. (2009). Models for individual oral health promotion and their effectiveness: A systematic review. *Australian Dental Journal, 54*(3), 190–197.

www.ingramcontent.com/pod-product-compliance
Lightning Source LLC
LaVergne TN
LVHW082333200926
848481LV00012B/3336

* 9 7 8 1 7 6 4 5 9 3 6 5 6 *